UNDER THE *Apple* TREE

UNDER THE *Apple* TREE

REBECCA BROCKWAY

Blue Ink Media Solutions

Under the Apple Tree

Copyright © 2024 by Rebecca Brockway. All rights reserved.

No part of this publication may be reproduced, distributed, or transmitted in any form or by any means, including photocopying, recording, or other electronic or mechanical methods, without the prior written permission of the author, except in the case of brief quotations embodied in critical reviews and certain other noncommercial uses permitted by copyright law.

The contents of this work, including, but not limited to, the accuracy of events, people, and places depicted; opinions expressed; permission to use previously published materials included; and any advice given or actions advocated are solely the responsibility of the author, who assumes all liability for said work and indemnifies the publisher against any claims stemming from publication of the work.

Printed in the United States of America
ISBN 978-1-64133-945-2 (sc)
ISBN 978-1-64133-946-9 (e)

2024.10.07

This book is printed on acid-free paper.

Because of the dynamic nature of the Internet, any web addresses or links contained in this book may have changed since publication and may no longer be valid. The views expressed in this work are solely those of the author and do not necessarily reflect the views of the publisher, and the publisher hereby disclaims any responsibility for them.

Blue Ink Media Solutions
1111B S Governors Ave
STE 7582 Dover,
DE 19904

www.blueinkmediasolutions.com

*This book is dedicated to
my daughters
Megan Rebecca Campbell and
Lauren Elizabeth Campbell*

*You are joy.
You are hope.
You are inspiration.
You are beauty.*

Reflections

One sun-drenched autumn afternoon, I knelt in the wet grass as I worked in my flower beds, planting spring bulbs. The moist dirt clung to my hands as I placed the last bulb in a freshly dug hole. I gently covered it with soil, and then I grinned, knowing that in a few months I would savor a sweet surprise as tulips, daffodils, and crocuses would dot my landscape. I breathed a sigh of satisfaction as I sat back on my heels and whispered, "Ah, this is the life." A gust of wind caught my hat, and as I held it to my head, my thoughts were suddenly flooded with past images and memories.

With eyes closed, I took a deep breath of fresh air and once again recalled the aroma of my mom's home-baked cookies as I walked through the front door at the end of a school day. I chuckled with delight as I recalled sweet words spoken by a toddler with lipstick smeared on her soft, ivory skin. I felt tears well in my eyes as I plucked from my memory the droning hum of the oxygen pump that came from my dying father's bedroom. I laughed out loud when the vision of my ex-husband appeared before me in his boxer shorts as he hunted for that pesky mouse, ski pole and Sears catalog in hand. My fears stirred as I relived the moment and recalled the reverberating sound made as a judge dropped his gavel on yet another broken marriage. And my spirits soared remembering when a soft-spoken truck driver took my hand and whispered, "Always."

I thought to myself, "What does it mean to have lived a good life?" Clearly, all I knew for certain was that living *a* good life was different than living *the* good life. I considered that living *a* good life was most likely fostered by applying restraint and following certain moral and ethical guidelines, a path to a purposeful journey. In contrast, I ascertained that living *the* good life was initiated with less reserve and most likely fed by one's demand for instant gratification. Make no mistake, I believed a person could live both, but there was, in my opinion, a distinction.

So, with these designations clear to me, I gathered my garden tools and rose to my feet. But, on the way to the garage, I pondered the personal question, "Have I lived a good life?" Although I assumed that I would offer a quick, silent yes to that question, I rather found myself in deep thought and contemplation. Had I been a good wife and a good mother? Had I been responsive and attentive? Had I been accountable, patient, and understanding? In every task and at every turn, for the remainder of the day, I played those questions over and over in my mind.

I realized that up to that point I hadn't found a definitive answer to those questions in any of the positive mental-attitude books I'd read, and the key hadn't been scribed on the ceiling in the delivery room as I'd *he-he-he*'d my way into parenthood. There had been no resounding discovery in that November issue of *Cosmopolitan* article that my friend had told me to read, either, even though she had underlined

Plato, G-spot, and dental floss. And I honestly hadn't found the solutions by listening to any talk-show host, no matter how profound the discussion or how high the TV ratings.

Consequently, I became frustrated and sought further clarification. I plopped down in a chair and decided to take a long, hard look at my life.

I deduced that I had had a good childhood, one with a stable and loving environment created by parents who were kind and nurturing. I had seemingly survived puberty and adolescence without any major consequence, and although I didn't have a college degree, I felt I was fairly intelligent and had received a decent enough education. I also had a pretty good head on my shoulders and had been fortunate enough, over the years, to have excelled in my employment opportunities. I had weathered the storm of a divorce, and my two beautiful daughters still cherished me, in spite of the breakup and the ensuing struggles. I had found love again, and I had two stepchildren who tolerated me, four dogs who worshipped me, and an ex-husband who *would* endure me, so help me, God!

My husband and I owned a beautiful and comfortably furnished home. We had nice vehicles, stylish clothing, good jobs, and genuine friendships. We had embraced change over the years and had adapted to laptop computers, cell phones, and debit cards. We basically had everything else a person needed in life, so what was I missing? What did I need to figure out?

I found it quite easy to acknowledge the good things in my life. I thought of my husband and how very much I loved him. I thought of the day we'd first met and how that encounter had changed my life, completely. My thoughts took me to the births of both of my daughters and how fulfilling and fascinating it had been to be their mother, to watch them grow and change right before my eyes. They had given me so many years of joy and happiness.

I considered the years that I had been fortunate enough to have shared my gift of singing: in church, at weddings, and with a band. I felt content that I had not only enjoyed my experiences as an entertainer but that I had benefited from them personally and professionally.

After much contemplation, I concluded that there must be a secret to living a good life and all I had to do was unlock it. Then, and only then, would I be able to set my mind at ease.

My attention quickly shifted, and I found my focus on some of those difficult experiences from my past—the ones that had caused me great worry and stress. As I dissected these memories, I tried to place them in perspective, and in doing so, I discovered that even my bad experiences had often fostered positive outcomes. Before this simple discovery, I had attached depressing and defeatist labels to these recollections, when in actuality all could be considered simply lessons learned. It seemed that the bad events had been just as valuable as the good ones, and combined, they had determined my journey on this river of life. They had certainly given my life substance.

With thoughtful prayer, in the quiet of my day, I began to come to terms with those painful recollections. I prayed that, as I grew older, the need to retrieve them would become less and less agonizing. The truth was, after a day of careful and quiet deliberation, I decided that I needed to find the secret to living my life well.

Much to my chagrin, I was already in my fifties! I was in the fifth decade of my life and the mother of young adults! I was a grown woman who thought I had most things figured out, and yet I couldn't get those crazy questions out of my head. Good grief! What had happened to my teens? My twenties? My thirties? And my forties? What had happened to my dreams? What had happened to my life? Why was this yearning now festering?

Maybe my life had merely unfolded while I was caught up in the middle of my unknowing quest for the secret. I often felt as though I was in the eye of a storm, determined to remain calm even though everything around me was spinning out of control. I often tried to slow down the chaos just enough to make it through until the next day or, God willing, next week. Often, in the wake of the squall, strife and struggle had ensnared me. Then, as quickly as the storm had erupted, time had shifted into another dimension, and still the secret had eluded me!

So, between the irritable heartburn, too little sleep, and recurrent bad-hair days, I became a simple American woman caught up in a race to unravel the secret. I didn't think that my future happiness solely depended on whether or not I could figure out the damned secret, but I felt the urge to further explore my life and to give definition and clarity to my past.

Later that week, my therapist suggested that I should begin a journal. In fact, she proposed that I record some of my life's experiences on paper. She baited me by telling me that some of the best authors began writing at the advice of their shrinks. Well, I didn't arrive at the decision to begin my literary journey solely because of the counsel to do so. No, my desire was merely fueled by my longing to find the answer to that burning question of whether or not I had lived a good life. My subconscious worked on me every chance it got. I considered, too, that it might be exhilarating to relive some of my life on paper, before I grew old and my failing memory began to lock away my past.

It's not that I had a life filled with intrigue and suspicion, nor was it a tormented or tortured life. No, it was quite the contrary. In fact, I thought I was pretty darned normal. But I believed that somewhere, locked away in the dark recesses of my mind, laid the answer—the secret.

So began my journey, as I searched for the one true thing that would convince me that I had lived a purposeful life. I spent months in reflection. I quickly jotted down yarns and then raced to my computer, only to find what a painstaking task it was to compile my memories into a comprehensible work. My years of perfectionism made my journey agonizing at times. I wrote, then edited, then re-edited my writing. Sometimes I added words, paragraphs, and sentences to what I thought was an already completed account, and then there were times that I deleted entire narratives altogether. It wasn't until my stories and reflections were concise and polished that I entertained the idea of publishing my work. Even then, there was the looming process of bringing the work to print.

Through this entire endeavor, I hoped to tell my story, the story of a life well lived. I wanted my daughters and my family to understand me. I desired to bring value to my memories and, in doing so, perhaps bring sunshine to someone's dark corner. I hoped that my stories would give encouragement and offer hope to someone else searching for answers to the same questions I had deliberated over.

You may not find *your* resolution here among my words entwined on these pages, but I sincerely hope that you will take pleasure in reading these most cherished memories. Maybe you, too, will be strong enough to face your past and realize the courage to begin again.

Reflections

The Lesson

Peering up through the branches of the old apple tree, I watched as billowy clouds stirred in the sky, changing shape and disappearing into the sea of blue above. Squinting to shield my eyes from the sun, I listened to him speak as we lay side by side in the moist green grass. Hanging on his every word, I reached out my small hand to touch the rough bark, tracing my finger around an imperfection that rose from the trunk's surface.

Chewing on a blade of grass, Daddy whispered into my ear, "Think about this, little one: you and I can enjoy the cool shade of this old tree because of one tiny little seed. It's just one of those miracles of life; that's the things that we don't think about often enough, and we should."

"What do you mean, Daddy?"

"Well, somebody had to plant the seed that started this old apple tree." He continued, "Yep! Most things in life have very simple beginnings. Someone plants a seed and then follows life's instructions."

"Daddy, what are 'structions?"

"That's *in*structions, little one. Well, they're directions, sweetheart. It's kind of like following a recipe when stirrin' up a batch of cookies or makin' a chocolate cake."

"Oh! Daddy, who wrote the instructions?"

"Well, I don't know, but I don't think you'll find 'em all together in any book—other than, ahh, I s'pose they're somewhere in the Bible, but I don't understand all that 'thee and thou' stuff. But I do know they were designed long before I was born, by someone very great.

"God?"

"Yep, I think so. Certain steps have to be followed in order to live and keep on goin' in the never-ending cycle of life. Little one, just remember this, live your life like you're responsible for keeping an apple tree alive. It really is that simple, ya know."

His speech became slower and more deliberate. "Think of your dream to do something special in your life as a small apple seed. From the time that single seed is planted, you must begin the process of carin' for it. To grow a strong, healthy tree, or to reach that goal in your dream, ya gotta water it and feed it. You have to feed your dreams; possibilities in life grow only with conscientious effort. And you know that you need to apply fertilizer too, right?"

"That stinky stuff?"

"Uh-huh. Bringin' up a tree is hard work and not always pleasant, just like livin' your life. *It's* gonna be hard work and not always easy goin'. In fact, sometimes things that happen in life will just sort of stink. But ya gotta keep the tree growin'. Keep it alive. Nurture it. And even after the tree is well established, there will be uncertainties that threaten, often challenges that ya must face in life. For example, a tree that's tall and fruit bearing has to have the branches pruned once in a while. It may lose its perfect shape, but you see sickly branches can stunt a tree's growth altogether, leavin' it sad and barren. Yep, cuttin' 'er back to where you find the healthy part will make for a stronger branch, a healthier tree, bigger and better fruit, and a dream that remains strong. Yeah, sometimes you have to cut away the dead parts of a dream. Forget about them. Move on."

"Daddy, if the tree is strong and healthy, it can give shelter to birds and insects, and me, right?"

"Uh-huh, you betcha. And you must keep your dream right there in front of you, so you can see it and tend to it each and every day of your life, because if you do, you will be the better for it."

"Like you and Momma? You grew up your trees good, huh? So, you can take care of me?"

"Yep, honey. That's right. A strong tree means the roots run deep, for a firm foundation and a sturdy shelter from the storms of life. You might still get wet from a downpour. But if you run for cover, you'll find that Momma and I will stand firm as the rain and winds sway our branches."

"Daddy, can I sit under your tree always?"

"Well, little one, there's a lesson for you in this answer. Just sittin' under my tree can teach you a lot about livin'. But you can't sit here forever. You have to make your own way in life, live your own dreams."

"But Daddy, I'm comfor-bull here. Why can't I sit here always?"

"Well, ya gotta be careful just how long you sit in any one place. And you have to be careful where you sit. Sometimes you can't tell if the grass is soggy until you discover your backside is already wet." He chuckled and continued, "And they'll be times when you won't be able to see the mess you're in until you get off your backside and figure out why you are where you are. Oh, my tree will always be there for you to find shelter under, but I can guarantee I won't always be able to keep you from sittin' back down in the same mess you just got up from!"

His voice softened as he said, "And ya know, little one, there will also be those times that my tree won't be as strong as it is right now. That's hard for me to say, but I'm a farmer, so I know that one day the turf under a tree can be as soft as silk, and only a few days later, it can be parched, dry, and scorched by the sun. One day a perfectly beautiful crop can be damaged right before your very eyes, and you can feel so helpless when you're up against the forces of nature and life's trials."

"What about the apples, Daddy? In growin' up a tree, where does the fruit come from, and what does it mean?"

"Well, it comes from the blossom, and it means you've given it lots of water and nourishment; the apples are the fruits of your labor."

"I don't know what that means, but I know that I've heard Grandma say that very thing."

"And the fruit will always hold surprises. You may take a bite of pure perfection and suddenly find a whole worm staring up at you—worse if you only find half a worm."

"Just half of a worm, Daddy? What happened to the other part?"

"Ummm, it's icky, are you—?"

"Oh, no, Daddy! I got it, never mind. That *is* icky!"

"Anyway, like I was sayin', the fruit may be sour or bitter, leaving an unpleasant taste on your tongue. Or, from time to time, the lingering taste can be forbiddingly sweet."

"What does that mean? I don't know what *that* word is, but Grandma says lots of things are forbidden, and so I think it means stay away from it!"

"Is that right? Well, forbiddingly sweet means that perhaps you shouldn't be enjoying the fruit so much, because there's still work to do, and if you stay too long and eat too much fruit, you'll end up with a bellyache. So do you understand now what that means?"

"I guess so. Um, and winter, Daddy? How do I keep my tree alive in the cold and snow?"

"When winter approaches, your tree will retreat to a dark place for a good sleep, only to be awakened by gentle rains and the return of the spring. Like spring, winter's just a part of the never-ending cycle. And that means that sometimes, even though your dream is still right out there in front of you, you need to rest. Then, when you're feeling refreshed, you start working again. The tree will blossom, and the bees will swarm, in celebration of new life."

"Daddy, how come the apple blossoms need bees? They kind of scare me because I don't want to get stung."

"Even in a seemingly perfect life you'll have to deal with some unpleasant critters. Why, without those pesky buzzers, there would never be fruit. Not havin' fruit doesn't mean the tree isn't still beautiful, but it just wouldn't have apples without the bees."

"Oh, yeah. The bees pollymate, right?"

"Well, somethin' like that. It's actually called pollinate."

"And robins can sit in my branches too, right, Daddy?"

"Yes ma'am, but you have to make room for the nasty old crows too. The melodies of life aren't always as sweet as the robin's song. You may have to deal with some naggin' old buzzard cawin' at you once in a while."

"Kinda like Grandma caws at you?"

"Yep! Heh, heh—you're a smart one, aren't ya, little one?"

Turning my attention back to the bump on the trunk of the tree, I asked my daddy, "What if my tree gets hurt? Will it cry? Will it bleed? Will it need a bandage?"

"I think trees cry, and when they get hurt, I think they bleed too. But see that bump on the trunk, right under your finger?"

"This one?"

"Yep. That's just an old scar. It gives the tree character, makes it different than any other apple tree—you know, unique. It probably did hurt when it was wounded, but it didn't stop growin'. It just healed itself over and continued to stretch toward the sun."

"And, Daddy—what happens if someone chops my tree down? What then? Will my tree die? What if somebody tells me my dream is stupid?"

Daddy reached out for my small hand and grasped it as he said, "Well, little one, the mere fact is that even though no livin' thing on earth can live forever, your tree will never *really* die. Because, ya see, over the years of livin', a tree produces many seeds. Some of those seeds will remain only as memories, but you'll plant some that will grow into magnificent new trees and then the cycle starts over, and over, and over. And nobody—and I mean nobody—has the right to tell you your dream is stupid."

"So, I'm kinda like one of yours and Momma's seeds, right? Was I one of your dreams?"

"Yep. And one day you'll sow some seeds and create memories and maybe even have your own children. After all, remember, you only need a single seed to begin again and keep your dream alive."

"That's nice, Daddy. I love you."

"Yep, I love you too, little one."

The Seed

I was born on March 26, 1957, on my sister Debra Jean's fifth birthday. She was hoping for a chocolate cake with pink frosting, ice cream, and a new doll. What she got instead was a red-faced, red-haired little bundle of crying *sister*. Born at two thirty-one in the morning, I weighed seven pounds, three and a half ounces and was twenty and a half inches in length. I, of course, don't remember anything about that day or about my homecoming from the hospital. But I can only imagine that Momma's focus in that early morning was on her labor and delivery and the significance of these statistics and *not* entirely on the little five-year-old making her birthday wish and blowing out her candles. I must have ruined Deb's birthday. Every birthday after that, for her *entire* life, would be shared with me, her little sister. The rudimentary comment from the masses was that we were twins, just five years apart! Yeah, like that was funny or even possible!

My other sister, Pamela Sue, was a couple of years older than I was. And then there was my brother, Philip Scott, who was born five years after me. Four children constituted a pretty normal-sized family back then, and a ten-year age difference between the oldest and the youngest was not uncommon.

My father, Kenneth Philip Clark, born July 12, 1930, was a handsome, sandy-haired, blue-eyed gentleman, and my mother, Betty Lou Smith Clark, born December 29, 1931, was a dark-eyed beauty. Married January 14, 1951, my mother and father were the perfect illustration of a happy marriage. They were an exemplary couple of the '50s—even the Cleavers paled in comparison.

Daddy would often hug and kiss Momma in our presence. She would giggle and respond with a smile and a warm embrace and then get on with her cooking or cleaning or whatever she was doing. There was no doubt that my momma and daddy were in love. There was no question that they loved us, either. They told us all the time, with their words and with their actions.

Daddy was a hardworking man, with a stocky frame and not an ounce of extra fat on him. He was a self-taught carpenter, an intuitive farmer, an excellent horseman, and a caring shepherd to his family. He had many other fine qualities, some of which I wouldn't recognize until my later years. My daddy was well respected in our community. His shy sense of humor endeared him to his family, friends, and neighbors.

A creature of habit, he was a predictable sort—a trait, I would learn, that is quite common in men. Daddy was up every morning at the same time, sat in the same place at the kitchen table, drank his coffee from the same cup, and smoked the same brand of cigarette for years. You could set your watch to the clanking sound of the milk buckets as he returned from milking the cows.

He did funny things, not intentionally funny, but nonetheless humorous. One day, while working in the pig barn, he stuck a pitchfork through the toe of his boot. He made it up the path to the house, pitchfork still lodged in his boot, as he feared the worst. He was convinced that he felt blood oozing between his toes. Yet, when Momma pulled the pitchfork out and removed his boot, it was discovered that the forks had missed his toes and foot entirely. Not a mark was on him. Momma teased him, and his face turned red with embarrassment.

He also tossed out malapropisms occasionally. He never could say the word aluminum. It came out "alunamum". As with the word linoleum, this was always mispronounced as "linomian". Then there was the time, when ordering breakfast at a local establishment, he asked the waitress for a "quickie" instead of quiche. We all laughed at this one, including him and when he laughed, his eyes would sparkle and his tummy would ripple.

He had quite a sweet tooth too! He used to take Momma's homemade chocolate pudding and sprinkle sugar on the top before eating it. Daddy's favorite reward for a hard day's work was Momma's lemon meringue pie with a cup of freshly brewed coffee. He believed tea was for sick folk and wouldn't dream of touching the stuff!

He doted on my mother, admiring her for her beauty and strength as a woman and a mother. Daddy would have walked through fire for her or for us.

Momma was exquisite! Tall and slender, with olive skin and flowing dark hair, she had the look of a Hollywood actress, beauty queen, or model. Her skin was smooth and flawless, and she had full, seductive lips, along with the most gorgeous legs of any mom I knew.

She was talented in so many areas of her life. Momma had a lovely singing voice, and she could play piano, not by following written music but by listening to tunes with a keen ear and then reproducing the song. She could plunk out the most marvelous ragtime piano you ever heard. She was an aspiring artist, taking pleasure in developing her talent to draw and paint. She taught church school for years and was a valued member of a group of churchwomen, the Toston Ladies Aid. She was a 4-H leader and volunteered for many jobs and positions within the community. She was also an excellent cook and seamstress, and I used to marvel at her creations.

When we were young, our momma spent many a late night creating the perfect Halloween costume or that new dress for the first day of school or Easter Sunday. She even sewed beautiful wardrobes for our dolls. In our teen years and beyond, she would piece together the most incredible prom and wedding dresses that one could imagine. She even made show-stopping western shirts for Daddy and Phil.

Momma taught me to organize things and how to cook and clean, in preparation for marriage and motherhood. She had a sensitive determination to be the best person that she could be. In my estimation, she *was* the best, and she was wise beyond her years. One thing that I truly admired in her was her dedication to my father. She was a good wife, a loving partner, and a treasured friend.

Deb, Pam, and Phil were all dark-haired and dark-eyed, like Momma. Deb was cute as a bug's ear—a tiny, petite thing. She had skinny little legs and arms and a misshapen ear lobe that just gave her unique character. She wore eyeglasses, because without them her left eye kind of wandered about as if it were taking a walk. The doctor said she had a lazy eye. Momma said she was special. She was a lot of help to Momma in the kitchen, and she was good to Pam, little brother, and me.

My sister Pam was beautiful, with soft, gentle eyes and a sweet smile. Momma always worried about her because she walked kind of pigeon-toed. She was always telling Pam, "Stand up tall, straighten your feet, and watch how you walk." Daddy would smile at Pam as she sighed. Her shoulders would go back, and she'd walk straight as an arrow, just until she was out of Momma's sight. Pam also had bad allergies and asthma. She had some real bad spells that scared all of us, especially Momma. Pam often read stories to us, and she was always up for a game of checkers or cards. She was kind and mellow and never caused much of a stir.

Phil was a handsome little boy, with wavy hair and a devilish grin. He was my daddy's namesake, and he was our prize! He loved to play trucks in the sandbox beyond the back door, and he adored accompanying me when I gathered the eggs from the chicken coop. He was like a little shadow and wanted so much to be big, just like his Daddy was.

I always felt a little different. I didn't look like any of my siblings. I frequently questioned Momma, "How come I look so strange compared to the other kids? Did you and Daddy adopt me or something?" Momma would shake her head and assure me that she remembered *exactly* where I came from. Besides, I looked like my daddy, all except the eyes. I had big, dark-brown eyes like my momma's, but bright red hair like my daddy's. I had pale skin, so pale that my veins showed bright blue from underneath. When kissed by the sun, my nose and cheeks would become dotted with freckles. Daddy used to say that freckles were special. I thought they were dumb-looking, but that didn't stop them from showing up, year after year!

Grandma Verna Clark, born July 19, 1904, was a slightly built lady with graying hair, sharp, striking features, and stunning blue eyes, just like my daddy's. She wore crisply starched housedresses and smelled of pungent perfumes. She was what my momma referred to as a "pistol." I don't think Momma said that in a disrespectful manner, but we all knew that Grandma was the boss of the ranch, and Momma was very aware of *her* place in the scheme of things.

Grandma Verna was, by all definitions, a busybody. She was a pseudo town crier, bringing news to the residents of the county. No, she didn't stand on the street corner with a bell and yell "oyez, oyez," but she was very adept at spreading information. Jokingly, it was said, "telephone, telegraph, and tele-Verna!" Most of her gossip was just nosy chatter: who had dinner with whom, and where; who had traveled this month and where; where did so-and-so get that new dress; and exactly how much did that hat cost? But some of her gossip and prattle was mean-spirited. At times, the words rolling off her tongue were like razor blades.

My grandpa, Walter Leslie Clark, was a quiet man who never said much. He was born December 13, 1890, in Little Hocking, Ohio. In 1911, at the age of twenty-one, he had come west to Montana and began working as a ranch hand in Broadwater County. In 1918, he had entered the service in the 89th Division of the First Army. After his discharge, he returned to ranching, and in October, 1925, he and Grandma married.

He was a hardworking man, with little time for rest and relaxation—as Grandma constantly prodded him. I loved to catch him in moments of rest, because that was a time when he would share interesting and funny stories about what it had been like when he was growing up. Those were authentic cowboy stories about wrestling cattle, trapping, and living off the land.

He had kind eyes, but there was a distant coldness about him. He didn't want to be called Grandpa, by gosh, by golly! In his assessment, he was not old enough to be dubbed a grandpa. We were instructed to address him as Walt. So, Walt it was! I once referred to him as Grandpa and was quickly reminded of his more appropriate title. It did confuse me a bit. If he lived with my grandma, how come I couldn't call him Grandpa?

The Seed

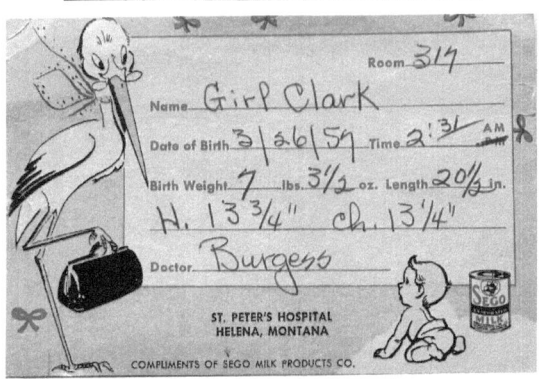

Rebecca Gay Clark - Age 8 months - photo December, 1957

UNDER THE APPLE TREE

*Wedding of Kenneth Philip Clark and
Betty Lou Smith, January 14, 1951.*

Kenneth Philip Clark and Betty Lou Smith

The Clark Kids

Left to right - back row Debbie, Pam
Left to right - front row Rebecca "Becky", Phil

Maternal Grandparents - Helen Smith and Stan Smith

Paternal Grandparents - Walter Clark and Verna Clark

THE SEED

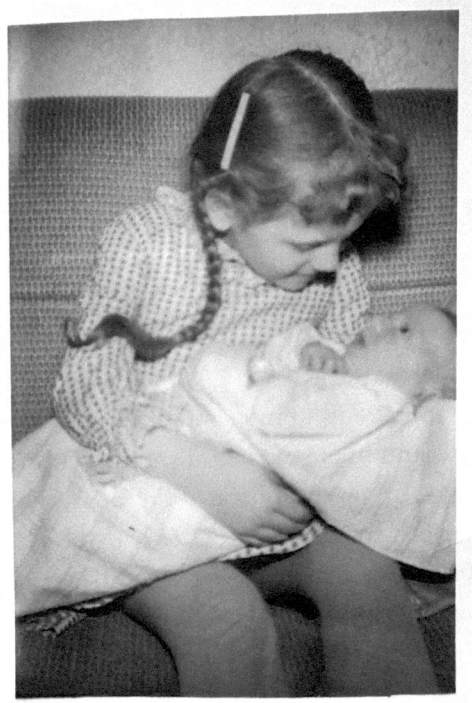

APR 1962

My "Prize"
Baby Brother, Philip Clark

Fertile Soul

My family lived on the Missouri River, near Toston, a small town in the heart of Montana cattle country. We inhabited one of the most picturesque of the farms and ranches in the Broadwater Valley.

My grandparents purchased the ranch from the McCarthys, and there was quite an interesting history surrounding our place. Toston, only a mile or so away, had been relocated to its current site in the late 1800s or early 1900s. Before that time, our ranch had been the town site. Toston had been named after Thomas Toston, first postmaster and first landholder of the rural estate. The small postal service had been operated out of a building on our ranch. Our house had actually been part of a hotel; the old barn had been the blacksmith's shop, and the "new" barn had been the other part of the hotel/boarding house.

Once small seedlings, the cottonwoods now towered over the lane down to the river. In earlier years my grandparents, Great-Grandfather Thomas, and my daddy had planted a shelterbelt of spruce trees on two sides of the town site. Four large spruces had been planted in the front yard of the big house, making a square sanctuary for play. As a child, I would spend hours inside the square with my blanket tent, acting the part of a settler in a newly discovered land.

The two-story farmhouse, or the "big house," was a haven to all who entered there. It was painted stately white with dark-green trim and had an inviting front porch, painted gray. Inside its walls, my parents had created a serene environment for our family. Our home felt safe and secure. To me it was paradise. In the shelter of our farmhouse, we were protected from the frosty chill of winter and the windswept days of summer.

The long staircase at the front entry was the kind that you saw in the movies of the old West, with a beautifully turned banister and a carpeted runner. Leading up to the bedrooms and bathroom on the second floor, the staircase was the most dramatic part of our home. When I was really little, Momma said, I would stretch out on my belly and slide down the stairs, going *bump-bump-bump* all the way to the bottom. As I grew older, I would play dress-up and descend the stairs like a princess in her castle, or slowly move down them like a saloon girl from the old *Bonanza* or *Gunsmoke* shows.

To the left of the entry was the parlor, our living room. That room was separated from the foyer by a set of magnificent wooden French doors. Through an arched opening was the combined family and dining room. The oak dining table and chairs were situated in a charming bay window, and a golden-framed mirror hung over the sideboard. The large brown-tweed sofa was woven with a delicate silver thread, and a round aqua-colored chair with an orange pillow occupied the corner. Sitting against a short wall between the parlor and the family room was an old black-and-white

Zenith television set. We had modest furnishings, but the house was pleasing—warm, and cozy.

Just off the family room was a huge pantry tucked under the staircase, with numerous shelves for canned and boxed goods. I spent hour upon hour playing store and rearranging the pantry. The shelves were always filled with food: store-bought goods and neatly stacked rows of home-canned delights. There were jars of homemade relishes and pickles, beans and carrots, and beets and tomatoes—just to name a few. To the left of the pantry was a gigantic storage closet, one of my great hide-and-seek hiding places. These were two of my favorite spots in the entire house.

To the right of the entry into the kitchen was a locked door. Behind it was Grandma's "secret room." It was a complete mystery to all of us. Hidden within those walls were all of Grandma's secret treasures. It was *her* private storage room. We were never allowed entrance. There was a window in the room, and from outside the house we would try to catch a glimpse of her mysterious cache. Climbing up on an old apple crate, we would teeter back and forth as we peeked through the rips in the drawn shade. We couldn't see anything! We didn't know what was concealed behind that door; it was puzzling. It was also a great source of frustration for my momma and daddy. We could have used the extra space, as we three girls shared one bedroom upstairs. But any time Daddy mentioned the room he was shushed.

I think Grandma was particularly fond of her squatter's rights within our home. It gave her an excuse to snoop every time we had company. We could always anticipate a room visitation when she wanted to know just who was visiting or exactly what was going on at our house. She would breeze in, unannounced, and say with a cackle, "I'm just putting something in my room; I won't be but just a minute. Don't let me interrupt anything!"

Grandma would open the door just wide enough to slip inside, and then the door would shut behind her. We'd hear some clanking and clambering from within the room and then weighted silence. Several minutes would pass, and the door would open, and out she would come. Turning the key in the lock, she would nod. Then, after jiggling the knob to make sure it was secure, she would drop the key in her housecoat pocket. She would linger in the house just long enough to make her presence known, and then out the back door she would go.

Our large kitchen was the gathering place for family and friends. Daddy had painted it a bold peach color that Momma had picked out, and she had made bright curtains for the windows. There were two sets of shelves on either side of the window over the kitchen sink, where Momma proudly displayed a small collection of her glass valuables. All the appliances and counters were lined up on the long outside wall, and the kitchen table sat in the middle of the floor. Behind a small cupboard door was a fold-down ironing table, not very well placed, either, I might add. By today's design standards, this would have been labeled a nonfunctional kitchen, but it was the heart of our home.

Our daily meals were served right there in the kitchen. We did our homework at the kitchen table and played board games there. We used our dining room table for holidays and special occasions only. I can remember many mornings that we sat at the breakfast table eating eggs, bacon, and toast and relishing the sun as it streamed through the window. We had a humble home filled with smells of freshly baked cookies and the sounds of laughter.

We always washed up for dinner in the bathroom that was right off the kitchen. A small painted stool, kept neatly under the sink, helped the little ones reach the faucet. Momma kept a small chest of drawers filled with fresh towels and linens. Next to the dresser was another locked door that led to Grandma's secret room.

Also off the kitchen was my third-most-favorite spot in the house: the screened-in back porch. There were cupboards out there, where my momma stored all kinds of stuff and my daddy hung his work clothes. It was a large porch, and in the summer, Daddy would take down the storm windows so we could enjoy the warm nights protected from mosquitoes and moths.

The steps were narrow and steep, and the door at the bottom creaked when opened. The basement was a scary place. The walls were whitewashed stone, and cobwebs hung from the low timbered ceiling. It smelled damp and musty. I didn't like to go down there by myself. Toward the back were the coal bin and the furnace, an old coal-burning dinosaur. The furnace grumbled and growled with the turning of the auger, sounding like a wild mountain lion in agony.

Momma's wringer washer was down there too, making laundry day an oh-so-pleasant event!" It also grumbled and growled and shook, but then, so did Momma on laundry day!

Daddy's cream separator was in the basement, as well. It was burgundy red, with bright, shining stainless steel. It was Momma's job to keep the separator clean and shiny. Every morning and every night Daddy would carry the fresh milk down the stairs and run it through the separator. The cream would go in the cream can and we would take the fresh milk to the refrigerator. We always knew when Daddy was back from the milking barn, because you could hear the purr of the machine as it worked.

Across the yard was the small house where my grandparents resided. White with aqua trim, it was a charming hodgepodge of a structure, which had originally been built for my momma and daddy. Grandma and Grandpa had bought three cabins at an auction and had moved them onto the ranch. One was the bunkhouse, Great-Grandpa Thomas had lived in one, and the other one became the bedroom of the small house. Later they had added a rectangular structure in the front, which became the bathroom, the living room, and the kitchen.

Momma and Daddy lived there quite comfortably for a while. However, with the arrival of three children, a switch in residence seemed the best possible solution for both families. My grandparents moved to the little house, and Momma and Daddy got the big house—that is, all but the secret room. Grandma had only agreed to move to the small house with the idea that she and my grandpa would build a new house soon after that.

I loved the arrangement. It was like having two home-style restaurants to choose from each and every day of the week, with different menus! At least one or two nights a week one of us would make the decision that Grandma had planned a much more appealing supper than my momma had. On the nights that Momma cooked creamed tuna on toast, Grandma's cooking usually beat Momma's hands down. Anything had to be better than that!

Our yard was extraordinary. It was huge! In fact, it was so large that we watered it with irrigation sprinkler pipe and mowed it with the farm tractor and hay mower. Before my daddy began to mow it with the tractor, however, Momma mowed the yard with an old push mower. She would start at one end, and by the time she was at the other end, it would be time to start all over again. There was a path worn right down the center of the grass from the back door of the big house to the well and the barn beyond.

Fifteen feet or so from the well was the most beautiful apple tree I have ever seen in my life. In spring, the breeze would carry the fragrance of the blossoms right up the worn path to our back door. The tree was a landmark on our place. Every year, on Easter morning, we posed under the apple tree, dressed in our finery, for the family snapshot. And every fall, our first-day-of-school photos were taken in front of the tree.

It was a comfortable spot, sitting under that apple tree. Under its twisted branches I could sit for hours, sheltered from the sun and the rain. Looking up through the thick tree limbs, I could see the robins as they greeted me with the first songs of spring. It was a favorite spot. From the apple tree I could see my momma through the kitchen window as she toiled. I could hear my grandma's singing as she hung wet clothes on the line, and I could hear my daddy as he whistled in the barnyard. I was in touch with my entire world from under my apple tree.

An Easter Sunday Morning

Rebecca "Becky", Pam, Debbie, Dad and Phil in front on his tricycle

Becky, Pam, Debbie, Mom and Phil in front on his tricycle

Plantin' Time

Daddy was the youngest of three children. After graduating high school, his sisters both left home and went to study nursing. Both married and set down their roots on the West Coast. Being an only son, Daddy remained in Montana to work the ranch with Grandma and Walt, or should I say, *for* Grandma and Walt. He was paid a modest salary and was provided with a house for his family. His dream was to someday own the place, his piece of heaven on earth. In my later years, I would learn that this modest salary barely provided for the necessities for our family, like clothing, shoes, and visits to the doctor.

We raised cattle, pigs, and chickens, so our freezer was always well stocked with meat. We always planted an enormous garden each spring and then harvested and canned the vegetables when they ripened, so we had plenty of food in the pantry. But there wasn't much of anything extra. We were poor by certain standards, but we were blessed in so many other ways.

Ranching and farming were hard work. There seemed to be little opportunity for idle time. The better part of each day, sun up to sun down, was spent in physical labor. There were cows to milk, chickens to feed, pigs to slop, land to till, horses to shoe, crops to harvest, and well, you get the picture.

I would surely have dropped from exhaustion if I had put in the hours that my folks did when I was growing up. I never remember my daddy sleeping much past five o'clock or six o'clock in the morning, unless he was sick. And I don't remember him being sick very often. Once in a while he would have bad headaches, diagnosed as cluster headaches. When that happened, he would lie down on the couch with a cold washcloth on his head. I remember, too, that his back would sometimes hurt and that would cause him to walk bent over. But he kept going. And my mom? Well, she would continue cooking, cleaning, and being Momma even when she was sick.

We were a hardworking family and made a cohesive team. Each of us had our chores to do and, in spite of the fact that we didn't much like to do them, those small responsibilities gave us a great deal of pride at a very young age. We made games out of some of our chores, which made the time fly by much quicker, and we sang songs while churning butter or sweeping the kitchen floor.

My folks were incredible role models. They taught us the rewards of hard work. A job well done was a job done well. Sometimes we would get that trip to the creamery for an ice cream cone, a Sunday afternoon fishing trip in the mountains, or an evening excursion to the local movie theatre, popcorn included! We didn't have a monetary allowance. My momma's and daddy's rewards were even better than money!

I so vividly recall the neatly tilled rows of our garden that we sowed each spring. We kids would walk along, stooping as we dropped the fragile seeds along each row. Daddy would come behind with the rake and cover up the deposit of seeds that we had so carefully placed. And every spring there would be cause for celebration when the first sign of tender green would pop from beneath the rocky soil.

Weeds were unwelcome intruders in our garden. Grandma was quick to educate us in proper identification—the difference between weeds and vegetables. We would spend many hours each week nurturing our garden: weeding, watering, and picking up a menacing rock here and there. The entire family enjoyed a favorite treat when the new potatoes, carrots, and peas were harvested and cooked up and then mixed together in a prepared cream sauce. One word describes it—delicious!

I always felt as if Grandma Clark loved me very much. But as I grew older, I became more aware that there was a feud brewing between my parents and my grandma. I don't remember Grandma being mean to us, her grandchildren, but more and more frequently she was making comments in our presence about things that didn't concern us; they were about private matters between her and my momma and daddy. I didn't understand this bickering, but I loved her and spent a great deal of time with her.

When I was just a second grader, she made me an honorary member of the Broadwater Flower Club. She taught me to appreciate the beauty and wonder of the outdoors. Nature, in her opinion, was a gift from God, from which we were destined to derive joy. We went on special trips to the mountains, climbing up hillsides, crawling over rocks and tree stumps as we searched for wildflowers and birds. She and I would pick small specimens as trophies, remembrances of our adventures. And we would always catalog our findings, which consisted of pressing the beautiful petals between the pages of her encyclopedias. When the flowers had been pressed and dried, we would glue them onto pages, look them up in one of my grandma's many flower books, and record the names of them and the dates that we discovered them.

I was even granted permission from the club members to enter floral arrangements in shows when I was only seven years old. My goal was to receive a purple or blue ribbon, but Grandma showered me with praise no matter what color ribbon my award was.

She cultivated ladylike qualities in me too, teaching me proper etiquette and manners. I accompanied Grandma to many of her friends' homes for tea and conversation—more appropriately, tea and gossip. I loved those times. And I loved Grandma's lady friends. They were so much fun to listen to!

Grandma was also instrumental in developing my love for music. She had a fine collection of seventy-eight- and forty-five-speed records, and I can remember sitting for hours and hours as I listened to the songs of classic artists like Jeanette MacDonald and Nelson Eddy.

She encouraged, or rather nagged, Momma and Daddy to provide us with a piano for lessons. Momma took a job selling Minnesota Woolen Mills clothing door to door in order to purchase the piano. It was a great sacrifice for her, but after many months she had enough money to pay for it. That beautiful piano commanded distinguished appointment in our living room and would become a source of education, pride, and entertainment in the years to come.

Grandma was a regular army sergeant when it came to music lessons, and she made sure that we practiced every day. My recollection is that she was kind of nasty in this role. She would *tap-tap-tap* the beat of the song on the piano, making me so nervous that a wrong note was inevitable. Then she would screech her discontent at the blunder. She expected perfection and gave me little room for error.

Momma acted as a buffer between my grandma and me. With the lesson over and Grandma gone, my momma would sit quietly by and listen to me as my little fingers searched the keys for the right notes. She would smile and give me a silent nod, letting me know that I was doing okay. Momma provided emotional bandages for my delicate, hurt feelings. She did all this while biting her lip and never saying a word.

Momma and Daddy never said bad things around us about Grandma or Walt, but I sensed that things were getting much worse every day. It was evident in their facial expressions. Momma and Daddy began arguing and fighting too, which was not typical for them. I would hear mumbles coming from their bedroom at night. The whispers sometimes became louder, and I would hear anger and fear in their voices.

I would often wait until the house grew quiet. Then I would sneak to their bedroom, open the door, and climb into bed between them. Daddy would stir and pull back the covers, and I would snuggle down in their warmth. Morning would come and everything would seem better.

I spent many a night cuddled up to my momma and daddy in their bed. Startlingly enough, they still managed to conceive my little brother. When he came on the scene, many things changed. For one, I was no longer the youngest and the center of attention. Even though my daddy worshipped his daughters, he had longed for a son.

Brother Phil's birth was a blessed event for Daddy and for a grandpa called Walt. I guess that, with the arrival of a grandson, the title of Grandpa was to be deemed appropriate. So, from then on, Walt became Grandpa Walt.

Deb, Pam, and I occasionally reverted to calling him by his first name only, but we were no longer admonished if just "Grandpa" slipped out. Funny how little Phil's entrance into our world changed everything. Grandpa Walt found new life in his grandson and a renewed stake in the goings-on of the ranching operation. His opinions became stronger, and he and Grandma began to have little spats. Daddy referred to their disagreements as the "struggle for the throne."

Grandpa Walt's health was soon threatened by a series of heart-attack events, and Grandma grew shorter of temper. Therefore, my daddy was under even more pressure to perform his duties. During that period of time, I recall that my momma worked side by side with Daddy in the months of harvest and with other responsibilities of ranching and farming. She not only did her regular chores as a housewife and mother but she cooked for the hired men and would don her dungarees, tie back her long hair with a bandana, and climb aboard the tractor, buck rake, or combine.

My sisters and I would make lunch for them, pack it all up, jump on our bicycles, and pedal to the field. The crew always delighted in the culinary experience of lunch break and would then resume their drudgery of harvest. We would pack everything back up and return to the house, where our domestic chores awaited us.

In Momma's absence from the house, my sisters and I were responsible for much of the cleaning and cooking. We didn't complain. It was just a fact of life. Grandma assumed much of the duty as caretaker for little brother, but at times we were responsible for that, as well.

Things always calmed down at the conclusion of fall harvest. Momma and Grandma worked long hours preparing and canning fruits and vegetables each season, the rewards of our laborious summers. The chickens, steers, and pigs would be butchered, wrapped, and waiting in the freezer, and my momma's focus would be on preparations for the holidays: Halloween, Thanksgiving, and Christmas.

Halloween was always special, and the party at the country school was a welcomed event. Being that we were rural folk, the nearest neighbor could be as close as a half mile or as far away as ten, so trick or treating was downright impractical. Round those parts, we would dress up in costume, load up the car, and head for the school. We delighted in the pageantry of the Halloween festival as we bobbed for apples and played hide-and-seek in the schoolyard under the harvest moon.

The Clark kids' costumes were always the envy of the party. Momma was a wizard! In our childhood years we dressed up in bunny suits, acted the part of Indian warriors and princesses, and galloped about in our cowboy attire. Halloween was a wonderful time, sprinkled with memories of carving pumpkins and munching on caramel corn.

The Thanksgiving holiday was always a big feast at our house. Momma and Grandma often combined their banner skills in the kitchen. We would wake early to the smell of roasting turkey, which had been stuffed by my momma's gentle hands at an ungodly hour of the morning. Daddy always picked out the largest gobbler, so it needed to be in the oven usually by five thirty or six o'clock in the morning.

Upon waking, we would scurry down the stairs to tune in the black-and-white television to channel 4 and to the Macy's Thanksgiving Day parade. It was a family tradition to crawl up on the sofa, cuddled in a blanket, and watch the parade in its entire splendor. We shouted out oohs and aahs as the exquisite floats became visible on our screen.

Dinner was family time, a time to reflect on the year and a time to give thanks and reverence to our Lord God for his provisions and blessings. We indulged, as my daddy would say, in "eats, treats, and sweets."

Holiday dinners at the Clark Ranch were edible delights. The Thanksgiving turkey was always roasted to perfection and was accompanied by all the trimmings! Momma's pumpkin pie was the best, with its fresh whipped cream and buttery, flaky crust.

After dinner, we would work together to clean up the kitchen and do the dishes. This was the time when all of us would break into song—well, all but Daddy. He would smile as he listened to the harmonious sound that filled our country kitchen. Singing always made the work go faster, and the work offered opportunity for us to exercise our vocal cords. Then we would play board games or put together a jigsaw puzzle as we waited for our food to settle. Sometimes Momma and Daddy would slip away to catch a catnap.

In the early evening, we would break out the leftovers for a snack before we tuned in to the long-awaited Thanksgiving special, *The Wizard of Oz*. We knew all the lines to the movie by heart. And, although we saw it every year, the wicked witch still terrified me!

Around Thanksgiving came another special event: the arrival of the Montgomery Ward catalog.

Early Photo of the houses and outbuildings, shops, barns, etc., of The Clark Ranch

All I Want for Christmas

"Momma, is it here yet?"

That was the question each and every year as we awaited the advent of the Christmas Wish Book, the Montgomery Ward catalog. We checked the mail with fervent excitement every afternoon.

"It's here! It's here!"

Oh, the catalog was wonderful! Climbing in my bed at night, I would page through the book as I made a mental list of all of the items I desired. On those pages were the most glorious dolls one could ever imagine. There were dolls that cried, dolls that wet, dolls that opened and closed their eyes, dolls with curly hair, and dolls that said "momma" when you tipped them just right. There were so many from which to choose.

I'll never forget the year I picked out the doll Pebbles, the baby from *The Flintstones* cartoon. She had red hair, just like mine, tied up with a plastic bone. Her little outfit was made of faux leopard fur, like that of a cave man. She was precious.

"Momma, this is what I really, really, really want! She is so cute! Can I ask Santa?"

Momma helped me write my letter to Santa. We addressed it to The North Pole and I carefully licked the postage stamp and placed it in the corner of the envelope.

Under the Christmas tree that year was my gift from Santa, the little Pebbles doll. We didn't get much, but we were always blessed, and our dreams for that special toy always came true.

That same year, Momma and Daddy gave us green metal fishing-tackle boxes filled with toiletries and special girly stuff. We each got the same thing, only in different colors. Included in each box were a new hairbrush and a shiny new comb. They were so pretty!

After all the gifts had been opened, we left the living room to help prepare for dinner. Deb, Pam, and I were in the kitchen when we heard Momma shriek from the living room. We ran in to find her standing in the middle of a scattering of small plastic pink, blue, and yellow bits. To my horror, she stood holding our once-beautiful new combs. They were now nothing more than mere skeletons. All the teeth were gone! Someone had broken out every tooth from each comb. Who would do such a thing?

Daddy bellowed, "Debbie, Pam, Becky? All right, which one of you did this?"

"Not me!" Debbie exclaimed.

"Me either!" Pam blurted.

"Phil?" questioned Daddy.

"Uh-uh, I dibn't dood it!"

"Becky, that leaves only you—what do you have to say?"

"But, Daddy, I didn't do it—honest! Maybe somebody else did it, but I didn't, I promise!"

"Well," he inquired, "and just who did?"

After specific interrogation of all, acting as judge and jury, Daddy dismissed Deb, Pam, and Phil. He motioned for Momma to leave the room, as well. I knew I was in deep trouble.

"Daddy, don't you believe me?" I begged.

He presented the facts as he saw them, "Deb didn't do it. Pam didn't do it. They were busy in the kitchen doing dishes. And Phil, well he's just too little to do something like that. I am concerned that you are telling your daddy a lie. You know I'll have to punish you if you don't tell me the truth. Well, what are you gonna tell Daddy?"

"I didn't do it, Daddy. Don't spank me, please."

He spoke very firmly as he said the two words, "Come here." At his request I crept toward him with my head down. With a grave look on his face, he said, "This is going to hurt me worse than it hurts you."

He turned me over his knee and whacked me a couple of times. His hands were huge; he wore a size-thirteen ring. Trust me, when that large hand connected with my little behind, it made a dreadful noise, and it stung like a January wind slapping across your face.

I was crushed—my daddy didn't believe me. And what was worse, somebody had lied! I ran up the stairs to my room and flung myself on my bed. The tears wouldn't stop. It was awful. It felt like hours before Momma came to comfort me. But she did. She held me as I sobbed. I was so angry, and I didn't understand!

When dinner was almost ready, we were all called to the table. I was rather quiet and guarded. I couldn't even look at my daddy. He had never spanked me like that before, and on Christmas Day! My eyes looked around the table at my sisters and my brother with a most discerning glare.

In the quiet of grace, with our heads bowed, my sobs could still be heard. My eyes were puffy and red, and I could not smile, even when Momma gave me an extra dill pickle.

We were well into eating our dinner when my sister Pam began to squirm. Then the tears commenced. "I did it! I broke the combs! I'm sorry I lied!"

I looked up with a horrified stare as I listened.

She continued, "I took my thumb and went *zip* down my comb, and the teeth just pinged everywhere! It made a neat sound so I *zipped* Becky's and Debbie's too! I'm really sorry, honest! Please don't be mad at me!"

I couldn't believe what I was hearing. I was the one with the sore, red welts on my butt. And she had the gall to say don't be mad!

But what I heard next was absolutely unimaginable, an assault to my senses! Daddy looked at her and said, "You're a good girl for telling the truth. Now, apologize to your little sister."

What's this? What about her butt? Was she not deserving of some punishment? I could have wrung her neck. And Daddy—what was he thinking? What about me getting an apology from him for the brutal whipping? Oh! Where was the justice? (I know I was a little melodramatic!)

Well, Pam did get her due punishment, but I have never forgotten that spanking. I don't remember any other spankings particularly well, and there *were* others prior to that, I'm certain. But I remember *that* one the most because I hadn't deserved it. I hadn't lied. I hadn't done anything wrong. I had told the truth. It hadn't been fair.

Daddy *did* apologize to me that night. As he tucked me into bed, he asked me to forgive him. He said he was sorry, and as he turned off the light and closed the door, I asked him, "Daddy, did it really hurt you worser than it hurt me? 'Cause it hurt me real bad."

The door closed quietly behind him. He never spanked me again.

A Good Watering

I must have really annoyed my sisters. They were fairly close in age and really didn't want to be pestered by a little creature such as I was! I flaunted the fact that *I* was "Daddy's little girl," 'cause I had red hair just like him and I was the baby girl. I wasn't really spoiled any more than they were, but in *my* mind, I was the queen.

Sunday mornings were frantic around our house. Momma would always wash our hair on Saturday nights, but we had to bathe the next morning. Church started early, and my momma and daddy hated to be late for anything, especially Sunday services.

We were fortunate to have two bathrooms, one upstairs and one down. Momma and the girls shared the upstairs bath, and Daddy and Phil were generally confined to the bathroom downstairs, next to the kitchen. Momma would fill the tub full of water and then it was a fight to see who got first dibs.

To be the last in the pecking order of bathing was not the best place to be. The water would usually be cold by then, and the bubble bath would be reduced to mere scum that floated on top of the water.

A Good Watering

Momma was almost always first, because she was fastest and she needed to get everyone else ready. When she was done bathing, war was declared. We would run to the bathroom, tearing off our pajamas as we ran, because whoever undressed first got to jump in next. Sometimes we shared the tub, but with three growing girls, things got pretty crowded.

I had the system down pat. I didn't like cold water, and I wasn't crazy about taking a bath in somebody's icky dirt and soap scum. I could always hear Momma drawing the bath water, and I would scamper up the stairs, run into the bathroom, and shut and lock the door behind me. Out of breath, I'd say, "Hi, Momma. Thought I'd come bisit ya while ya taked a baff."

She would smile as she slipped down in the warm bubbles.

I'd strip naked, climb up on the toilet seat, and lean on my little elbows to chat. "Do ya need yer back squbbed, Momma?"

Momma would nod her head, yes, and welcome me to join her. She'd scoot forward and I'd step over the side of the tub to wiggle in behind her. She'd hand me the washcloth and I'd wash her back. We would often sing or hum a tune as the girls pounded on the bathroom door from the outside. I'd smile and Momma would rise from the tub and shake her head as she rinsed my lathered body. Well, my momma always did say the early bird gets the worm!

I'd step from the warm water and she would envelop me in a soft, warm towel. She'd kiss me and say, "Now, go and get dressed, and tell your sisters it is bath time."

I would prance into the bedroom and say in my snotty little voice, "Baff time, guhls. Betto huwee!" They would glare at me as they walked by. Over the years, I'd been pretty successful in developing my system of bathing privilege.

It was Easter Sunday morning, and Momma was particularly fussy about how I looked that day. That year she had made us matching dresses that were orange-and-white gingham. Deb's had large checks, Pam's had medium checks, and mine had tiny checks. They had full, twirly skirts and delicate lace at the neck and sleeves.

A big bow was fashioned in the back and tied at my waist. My hair was pulled up with matching ribbon, and auburn ringlets cascaded down to the middle of my back. I was stunning and I knew it—and I wanted my sisters to know it too!

They were still in the tub when I strutted in with my nose in the air. "I'm ready and you're not!" I chanted.

I could tell they were about as fed up as they could be. Yet, their voices sounded sweet as they said, "Come over here, Beck, and sit down while we finish our bath. Sit right on the edge of the tub and talk to us."

With my little head cocked, I sauntered to the tub, climbed up, and perched on the edge. My skirt, with its petticoat underneath, made a swishing sound as I sat. I folded my little hands in my lap and proceeded to mock them.

"I'm ready and you're not. I'm ready and you're not."

With my nose in the air, I didn't even see it coming. In the blink of an eye, they had pulled me in. I sputtered and coughed and kicked and squealed. With one swift movement they dunked me! I was drenched! I was a mess!

Momma hollered from the foot of the stairs, "What are you girls doing?"

"*Waaaaaaa!* Momma, look what they did to me!" I stood at the top of the stairs, dripping wet, bawling my eyes out.

Momma gasped as she ran up the stairs. "What happened to your little sister?"

Deb explained, "We don't know Momma. She was sitting of the edge of the tub talkin' to us and she just … slipped in."

Pam concurred. "Yeah, she just slipped right in, Momma."

"Rebecca Gay Clark! What am I going to do with you?" Momma asked as she grabbed my arm and hurried me into the bedroom. I heard giggles coming from the bathroom. Momma never heard a thing except the ringing in her ears as she impatiently peeled the soggy clothes off me. I tried to explain to Momma that my sisters had pulled me into the water, but she wouldn't hear of it.

I was the last one ready that day. My new dress was soaking wet, so I had to wear an old one that didn't match the other girls'. My hair was wet, in ugly old pigtails, and my bangs looked stupid. I barely even smiled in the photo under the old apple tree. I couldn't even wear my new black patent leather shoes because they were too wet and they squeaked when I walked.

Later that afternoon, during dinner at my aunt's house, she asked me if that was my new Easter dress.

I looked down at the floor as I said, "No, but I have one; it's just at home drying."

I knew I hadn't just slipped into the water, but I was outnumbered two to one, and neither one of my sisters was going to tell the truth. It wouldn't be the last time that my sisters got the best of me, either.

It was years before Deb and Pam finally admitted to our momma and daddy that they had, in fact, pulled me in. Why did they do it, you ask? I was being a little brat. I was the bratty little sister, and they had had enough of me on that day. They never intended to completely drench me, but when it happened, they made a pact that they were not going to tell the truth. As adults, we laugh about it now. I remember that Easter Sunday as if it were yesterday.

Bath Time

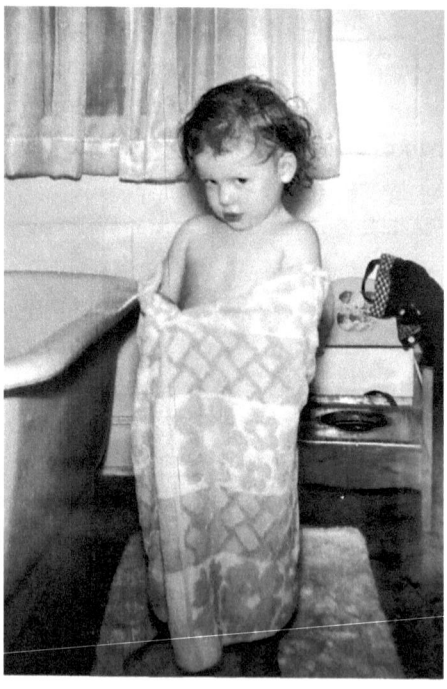

Photo of me

Seeds of Higher Learning

When I was old enough to attend school, I recall my momma sat me down and explained how very important it was to be courteous to my teacher. "Remember," she said, "always be polite and *listen* to what the teacher instructs." As simple as that request may sound, those were some of the most beneficial words of instruction I have ever received.

We didn't have kindergarten at our small country school. It was just expected that a first grader would be able to count to ten, know the primary colors, and be able to identify certain pictures of animals, objects, and such. Well, my momma and my grandma certainly made sure that each of us knew the basics long before we began attending school. Heck, I think I even knew how to write my name and count to fifty, and I certainly knew my colors!

There weren't many students in our school, either. I think at any given time there were no more than twenty students in all the grades combined, first through eighth grades. Well, that sometimes changed during the harvest season, when the migrant workers sent their children to school while they were working in the fields. Anyway, it was your typical small, rural school.

A two-story structure, the Toston School stood on a hill. It was white with a red roof and a bell tower. The large brass bell rang every morning, beckoning the children inside for class to begin; at mid-morning, signaling the end of recess; at lunchtime; and then again at the close of day.

On one side of the schoolhouse was an enclosed fire-escape slide, a source of entertainment to all the schoolchildren, young and old. We used to walk up that old fire slide, and when we got to the top, we'd turn around and slide down.

There were two classrooms on the main floor and both a front and back foyer, where we hung our coats and kept our snow boots in the wintertime. A bathroom for the boys and one for the girls were found off the front foyer. I remember the granular pink soap that dispensed from metal containers above the sink, how it smelled, and how dry my hands felt after I washed them.

Directly across from the lavatories was a staircase that led to the upper level. Across from the upstairs classroom was a small office for the teacher. That's where the mimeograph machine was kept, along with the typewriter and the telephone. Behind a third door upstairs was the school auditorium. We even had a small stage for our school plays and Christmas programs.

In the back of the large downstairs classroom was a small alcove, where the library was situated. It really wasn't a library. It was just the smallest of spaces, but there were built-in shelves, so that's where we put our collection of books and reference materials.

The playground was no more than a few patches of grass and lots of dirt and weeds, but we had a swing set, a slide, a merry-go-round, a teeter-totter, and giant strides. Another building, where the PTA and the school board met, divided the playground into two sections. There was a grassy area on one side of the PTA building, where we sat in the shade and ate our lunches as we watched the boys practice their jumps in the sawdust pit.

My momma was a member of the PTA, and my daddy was on the school board too. They always hired good teachers, or at least I thought they were good ones. I remember most of their names. Let's see, there were several: there was Mrs. Foster, Mrs. Stalcup, Mr. Armstrong, and Mr. Sample.

Mrs. Foster, my first-grade teacher, was wonderful. She was so kind and truly enjoyed teaching. She was pretty, with red hair, just like mine. She played with us on the playground and read to us each and every day. Yes, Mrs. Foster loved to read and encouraged us to do the same.

I remember, in particular, one book that she read to us. The title was *Rebecca of Sunnybrook Farm*. I hated that book! All of the students teased me; every recess they chanted, "Rebecca, Rebecca of Sunny Brook Farm—ridin' her pig, ridin' her pig!"

I went home and told Momma that I was glad she and Daddy hadn't named me Rebecca. She smiled and said, "Well, what do you think your name is?"

"Becky," I exclaimed. "And I'm sure glad it's not Rebecca!"

Another one of my very favorite teachers was Mr. Armstrong. His wife taught the first, second, and third graders, and he taught fourth and fifth. Mr. and Mrs.

Armstrong drove every day from Townsend, eleven miles, to teach at our little country school.

Mr. Armstrong was brilliant and wise, kind and thoughtful. He loved to challenge our minds, to encourage us to strive to be better tomorrow than we had been the day before. He loved the English language, both the spoken and the written word. He had passion for knowledge and teaching. He allowed me to experience learning in the highest degree.

Mr. Sample was another one of my memorable teachers at the Toston School. His wife was also a teacher. The year they came to Toston, she taught the first three grades and he taught sixth, seventh, and eighth grades. He was a tough disciplinarian, but I really learned from him. He brought to our little school some of the most innovative teaching methods I have ever seen. He stretched our minds and sped us along in learning as we gleaned knowledge from his experiences and techniques.

We had wonderful school programs for different holidays and special occasions. Our Christmas program was one that we diligently worked on for weeks and weeks. We usually had a Christmas play or pageant, and that always included singing. But aside from singing, one of my favorite times was Friday afternoon, because that's when we were allowed to do art projects.

I recollect one particular Friday afternoon; I was having one of those days. The boys had been teasing me all day. I had gotten three problems wrong on my math test, and one of my classmates had thrown my geography map in the dirty snow. But it was Friday, and tomorrow I would be able to play and read whatever I wanted.

Immediately following the afternoon recess, Mr. Sample, knowing how much I loved art, asked, "Becky, how would you like to lead us in art today?"

No way did I want to stand up in front of the entire class, just to have that classmate mock me! So, I said, very politely, "No thank you, Mr. Sample. I don't think I want to do that today."

Shocked that I would say no, and a little irritated, I might add, he shrugged his shoulders and said, "Well, class, let's all thank Becky. We won't be having art this afternoon. Let's take out our science books and have a quick review, and then we'll take a quiz."

All eyes were glaring at me. I was dead meat! I heard whispers and sneers as I walked to the front of the room to sharpen my pencil.

"Thanks a lot, Becky! Just because of you, we don't get art today!"

I shuffled back to my desk as the tears pooled in the corners of my eyes. I slumped in my seat and buried my face behind my science book.

When Mr. Sample excused us for the day, he motioned for me to sit in the back foyer until he talked with my mother. I can remember when my momma walked into the school that afternoon. She walked over to me as I sat on the bench with my head down. Lifting my chin with her finger, she questioned, "What's wrong, sweetheart? Did you get into trouble?"

I was just about to answer, when Mr. Sample appeared in the doorway and told Momma that he wanted to speak with her. She walked into the classroom, and I could hear them talking through the open door.

Mr. Sample began, "Mrs. Clark, Becky was disrespectful this afternoon. When asked to do something, she said no."

Momma responded, "Well, exactly what did you ask her to do?"

He replied, "I asked her if she would like to lead us in art, and she said no thank you!"

Momma took a deep breath and spoke. "Mr. Sample, Becky might not be a perfect child, but one thing I know for certain: she isn't disrespectful. You asked her, didn't you? Well, Becky simply answered. Don't punish her for making a choice and giving you an honest answer!"

Not even waiting for a response from Mr. Sample, Momma commanded, "Becky, get your things, and let's go home." Momma turned on her heel as she tipped her head in respect.

Later that evening, she explained how Mr. Sample might have thought I was being disrespectful. She said to always think before I say things so as not to hurt or anger someone unintentionally.

Boy, was that a hard lesson. But, gee, my momma really told him!

Bad Seed

Springtime came, and once again we welcomed the return of the bluebirds and robins and the buzz of the bumblebees as they gathered golden nectar from the blossoms of the apple tree. We had gotten pretty bored being captive in the house because of the winter snow and icy spring rains. We were always glad when warmer weather beckoned us to play outside once more.

An adventure to the barn and corrals seemed like a perfect way to spend an early spring Saturday afternoon. My cousin from town was visiting, and I was going to show this "city slicker" the ropes. First, we headed off to the barn where Daddy was working. Surely, we could find some trouble to get into if we just looked long and hard enough.

Daddy had built a network of corrals out of railroad ties and board planks; it was a maze of spaces connected by gates and well-planned corridors. The gates were constructed from heavy timbers that swung on stout metal hinges. We were constantly told not to stand on or swing on the gates.

On this particular sunny afternoon, my cousin and I were swinging on the large gate to the milking barn corral. We would unhook the gate from the lock and jump on. It would swing around and then smack the side of the barn. We would then jump off and pull it back around to catch another ride.

We laughed and giggled as Daddy walked by and said, "Hi kids! What ya doin'?"

Wow! He hadn't said a word about swinging on the gate—not one word. But I knew I shouldn't push my luck, so with the next ride complete, we pulled the gate back to its cradle and slid the latch down. Then on to the "new" barn we went.

The new barn was actually split off from our house, the old boarding house; it had been moved to its new location. We used it as our tack room. The door slid open to reveal the saddles, halters, and bridles, all very neatly placed.

There was a bag of rock salt in the corner. We grabbed small pieces of salt, stuck them in our mouths, and headed up the ladder steps to the loft.

In the loft were three old school desks and a large chalkboard. A few old textbooks were strewn about. We would often come here and play school for hours. Go figure! We spent our weekends and many of our summer vacation hours playing school!

There was a small window at the end of the barn, positioned perfectly over the stoop below. We would climb out onto the roof that covered the porch and sit there, taking in the sights and sounds of the barnyard. We had been repeatedly told not to climb out the window. It was dangerous. We could fall.

On this particular sunny afternoon, as we sat on the roof, Daddy drove by on the tractor. As he bounced by and waved, with a big smile, he yelled, "Hi, kids! Whatcha up to?"

Unbelievable! He hadn't said a word about us being on the roof, either. We sat there a bit longer, thinking: this is just too easy. Is there not something we can get into trouble with? Hurriedly we climbed down the ladder, in search of another adventure.

Grandpa Walt was working on a piece of farm equipment in the shop. We said hello as we wiggled between the grain bins and the Quonset hut.

Whoever built the shop must have been thinking of us when they placed the three metal grain bins so close to the Quonset. You see, we could climb up the bins by leaning our backs on the Quonset and stepping on the metal ridges, inching up the side. Once we made it to the top, we would slide down. We weren't supposed to do that either, but we did.

On one trip around one of the grain bins, I noticed that the door to the bin was ajar. I pulled it open to reveal the secret inside. It was filled with grain of the most incredible color I had ever seen. It was sort of an iridescent pink. I called for my cousin to come and look. It was such a beautiful color, and we both agreed that it looked like fun.

Grandpa Walt found us, only minutes after we had crawled into the bin. He grabbed us both by the arms and yanked us up from our "quicksand" fun. Terrified, we stood and stared at him. The tone in his voice told me we were in trouble.

Not that there weren't other dangers in playing in the grain bin, but the distinct danger here was that this was treated grain. It had been sprayed with a chemical and was poisonous.

Grandpa called to my daddy to come quick. When Daddy came around the corner of the Quonset, I saw the look of concern on his face. He scooped us both up, one under each arm, as he headed for the well.

Within seconds my eyes began to burn, and my skin felt as though it were on fire. He doused us both under the spigot, frantically trying to wash the poison off our bodies. We were both crying as Momma raced down the path from the house to the well. She saw the pink on our skin and clothing. There was the look of horror on her face.

Our eyes puffed up like wieners cooking on a grill. Our skin developed huge bumps that burned and itched. We could taste the poison on our tongues for hours afterward, just from breathing the dust. We both cried. I felt awful. And, sure enough, we got in trouble. I never would do such a stupid thing again, and pink would *not* be my favorite color, *ever!* Well, at least not until I developed a thing for pink flamingos.

Nine Lives

Since the time I was a small child, I have always held a special place in my heart for God's creatures, animals of all kinds—that is, all except spiders and box elder bugs. I even had a pet earthworm once, named Sam. I loved life on the ranch, being around the animals, and the wonder of life itself.

I used to ponder what it would be like to be totally dependent on someone else to take care of you. On the ranch we took care of the cows, horses, and pigs, and they, in turn, took care of their young. I did not take lightly my responsibility to feed and water the pets or take care of the chickens—although I thought the chickens were the dirtiest and most stupid creatures on the face of the earth! How else would they survive if we didn't take care of them?

I'll never forget the first time I saw a cow give birth. It was the most unbelievable thing I had ever seen. The miracle of birth was spectacular. I watched in awe as the mother nudged her newborn baby to stand on those wobbly little legs. Soon the calf would be running and jumping in the fields. I remember my daddy always said, "Never get between a cow and her new calf. They can get pretty mean when they feel threatened." I wondered if that's how Momma felt about Deb, Pam, Phil, and me.

One of the places I loved best on the ranch was the barn, because that's where most of the cats hung out. It was a pretty normal thing to have several barn cats. They kept the mouse population down. I loved them. When my daddy milked the cows, he often squirted the warm milk into the mouths of hungry, playful kittens as they watched with curiosity. It was always a special event when one of the momma cats gave birth to a litter. It was sometimes hard to locate the mom and her babies, but when I did find them, I sat for hours and held the little kittens. Eyes closed; they would squeak as they searched in the darkness for their mom. They were so little and helpless as they lay in their secret place, where they nursed and grew strong.

One day, some friends gave us a new barn cat. According to them, he was a wonderful mouser. He was young and spunky and would be a welcome addition to our older family of cats. He was a beautiful cat, black and white, with snappy blue eyes. We brought him home, and to test his incredible mouser capabilities, Daddy went downstairs to the basement to see whether the live trap he had placed there had any captives. Sure enough, there was a mouse in there. He brought the trap upstairs and took it outside, where he proceeded to let the mouse free. Our new cat took one look at the mouse and ran in the other direction. The mouse ran back into the house through the open door, and the cat went up the tree. Back down the stairs went the mousetrap, and up the ladder went my daddy to get the cat out of the tree. Hence the cat was christened Dumbbell. Our newly acquired "wonderful mouser and barn cat" became a back-door cat that thrived on table scraps and love.

Momma sold cream to the creamery in town for making ice cream, and she saved all her earnings for something special. One year, with the money she had saved, she bought Daddy a new, comfy, down-filled coat with a fur collar. It was a handsome coat, and my daddy was so proud of it. One cool fall day, Daddy asked all of us if we had seen his coat. He hadn't worn it but a couple of times, and it was no longer hanging in the closet on the back porch, where he had left it. I looked down at the floor as I explained, "Well, you see, Momma and Daddy, Dumbbell was cold, and so I made him a bed." I led them out the back door and to the caragana hedge. There, among the fallen leaves, was my daddy's new coat, with the perfect indentation of a curled-up, sleeping cat. A trip to the dry cleaners and the coat was as good as new. After that, my momma gave me an old blanket to use for Dumbbell.

One afternoon, as I walked out the back door with a pan full of table scraps, I was surprised when Dumbbell did not meet me at the door or trip me as I walked to the hedge to put food in his dish. Later that evening, I found him huddled under the garden cart. He was ill, almost lethargic, and he gave no resistance as I picked him up and headed for the house. With tears streaming down my face, I begged Momma to make him better. She took my cat from my arms and carried him down to the basement, where she made him a soft bed next to the washer. She left me to sit by him while she went upstairs to fix him a tonic. Returning a short time later, she and I coaxed Dumbbell to drink the potion of warmed milk spiked with aspirin. She said that we would check on him in the morning. I said good night to him as we turned out the light and climbed the steps.

The next morning, we found Dumbbell sort of sitting up, leaning against the washer. One would have taken him for a stuffed kitty, except for the loud snoring. We tried to rouse him but had no luck. We checked on him several times that day and found no change. For the next three days, the only movement from Dumbbell was the rise and fall of his chest as he slowly breathed. Several days later, he woke up and was back to his old self, tripping my momma as she carried laundry to hang on the clothesline.

Several weeks later, Momma took our little dachshund to the vet, because he was having back trouble. The vet said he needed to give him some pain pills.

Momma asked him, "What about aspirin?"

The vet said, "You never want to give an animal much aspirin."

With concern, Momma inquired, "Well, say you gave a cat six of them. What would that do?"

"Well, Mrs. Clark," he said, "You'd have yourself a dead cat!" Momma explained what had happened. His eyes lit up as he shook his head and mumbled something about a cat and its nine lives.

There always seemed to be an exchange of cats from one neighbor's farm to another. Any time a fella's barn cat population exploded, he just gathered up as many as he could catch, threw them in a gunnysack, and headed for the neighbor's field. Just within a comfortable distance from the neighbor's barn, he'd turn the cats loose. Cats would go everywhere, but you knew it had been a successful exchange when the majority of them took up residence in somebody else's barn.

Daddy and Momma tried this once with our excess number of kitties. I was horror-stricken to find out that my friend Dumbbell was in that sack. Reluctantly, Daddy opened the top of the sack to let him out, and cats jumped everywhere, headed in every direction. Most of them headed right back to our barn—all except Dumbbell, of course. He headed for the house and took his rightful place once again at the back door.

After one of these nighttime exchanges, we inherited a yellow cat with eerie green eyes. He had a nasty disposition and picked fights with most of the other cats. He, too, thought that living at the back door was a step up from the barn. Little did he know that he was invading "tough cat" Dumbbell's territory and that my momma had zero tolerance for a cat that hissed at us and fought with Dumbbell. The last straw was when she saw it carrying a dead bluebird. Daddy decided it was time to get rid of the mean yellow cat. He grabbed his .22 rifle and headed for the back door. When he returned to the house, Momma guessed that the deed had been done and told him to go and dispose of the dead kitty so that we wouldn't see it. He agreed and went back outside, only to return minutes later with a very puzzled look on his face.

"It's gone, Lady," Daddy said.

"What do you mean, it's gone?" Momma questioned.

"I mean the cat's not there. That's what I mean!" Daddy confirmed.

Weeks went by with little thought to the disappearance of the nasty yellow cat's dead body. Much to my momma's and daddy's surprise, however, he showed up again, very much alive—but with a new permanent crease on the top of his head. Evidently, my daddy had just grazed him with the bullet and probably knocked him unconscious. Daddy figured that if God saw fit to let the little thing live, he could too. The incident actually changed the cat's personality for the better, and he became one of the best barn cats we ever had. He never did hang around the back door again, though!

As I mentioned, we had a little dachshund. His name was Beauregard. At times I felt as though he had nine lives as well—or at least he wished he did—like the time he somehow climbed up on the picnic table and dragged an entire barbecued turkey off the table and into the bushes. Now, if that wasn't the silliest thing you ever saw—a little dog dragging something twice his size! Talk about your eyes being bigger than your stomach! Needless to say, Daddy was very unhappy. The thought of eating hotdogs rather than that turkey did not excite him. But we all laughed anyway.

Beauregard wasn't exactly the smartest dog on the planet. One of our favorite television shows was *Lassie*, and although Beauregard had never demonstrated the talents of Lassie, we still thought that he knew exactly what we were talking about and that he would instinctively save the day if we were in danger or trouble. Well, that was not the case.

On one occasion, Daddy hollered out from the barn to Phil, who was swinging on the gate. "Phil, there's a skunk in the barn. Run to the house and tell your momma to bring the 22."

"Okay, Dad," he answered.

Five or ten minutes passed, and Daddy heard the gate swing against the barn once again. "Son, did you run and tell your mom to come with my rifle?"

He responded, "No, Dad. I sent Beau."

Needless to say, Beauregard didn't save the day. The skunk sprayed Daddy, and Daddy sprayed Phil with some well-chosen words.

Happy Trails

One of my earliest memories is of sitting on the back of a horse—okay, so it was a pony! Daddy purchased an older Welsh/Shetland cross from a nice man by the name of Mr. Wall. Princey was black and white, with a star marking on his forehead. He was a right stubborn pony too, with a mind of his own. But he was my very best buddy.

These days, kids come home from school and turn on the television or log onto the Internet and sit in front of a computer all night. In my childhood days, I grabbed my bridle and saddle and opted for a horseback ride. I was still too little to cinch the saddle tight enough, so I asked Daddy or Grandpa Walt to help me. They cinched up the saddle, gave me a boost up, and I was on my way.

Princey couldn't stand a bar in his mouth, so my daddy fashioned a special bit that suited him and fit snuggly under his chin rather than in his mouth. That gave him freedom to eat as many apples as his tummy could handle on a late summer afternoon. He was a spoiled little guy but gentle as a lamb.

Princey loved to run. We would walk slowly to the gate under the cottonwoods. I'd jump off, grab the reins, and open the gate. His little ears would perk up when I led him through. He knew we were headed for a run down by the river. Daddy and Momma were very clear about our jaunts to the river. We were to stay away from the riverbanks and keep out of the alfalfa field. After we'd gone through the gate, Princey's walk would turn to a trot, and soon we would be galloping into the wind. I would feel freedom then, in that *Big Valley* sort of way. My pigtails would bounce up and down with each snort from my little horse. We would slow to a trot once again, turn around, and head back toward the gate. The sound of the river would be muffled by the squeak of the leather saddle against my blue jeans. The smells of cow manure and sweet grass would fill the air. I would feel that I *was* Audrey and I *was* riding a fine steed in my Big Valley. I *was* a western belle and an accomplished horsewoman!

I would be awakened from my daydream by the sound of the dinner bell. Princey and I would go through the gate and trot to the new barn, where my daddy would be waiting with a smile on his face. "Good ride there, little one?"

"Yep, Daddy; it was the best."

He would hold the reins while I swung down from my steed, and then he would help me remove the saddle and blanket. He would hand me the curry comb and pat Princey on the backside before he accompanied us down the hill to the corral. We would open the gate, and I would give my buddy an affectionate stroke under the chin and a kiss before I slipped the bridle off and turned him loose. He would whinny and throw back his head as if to say thanks. And off he would gallop with his tail up, through the gate to the pasture beyond.

The time approached when we would be driving the cattle to the summer pasture, up Dry Creek. Daddy and

Grandpa Walt were both incredible riders; they'd be in the saddle for the long trek from sunrise to sundown. Deb and Pam would trade off riding, because Deb would get tired and Pam had allergies and asthma and had to be carefully monitored. Phil and I usually rode with my momma in the stock truck, as I was too little to herd, and Phil was just a little kid. Momma was scared of horses. You couldn't get her on a horse! To her, horses were unpredictable creatures. Her opinion was that God just didn't mean for man to crawl on the back of an animal. But it worked out okay, because somebody had to drive the stock truck to bring the horses back at night, and she always packed a cooler and picnic basket for lunch and snacks.

I recall that one evening in particular the walk to the house was very special. Daddy had been watching my riding skills develop and mature. This day, Daddy had said, "How would you and Princey like to help take the cows to pasture this year?"

I jumped up and down and ran round and round my apple tree! That was the most exciting thing that had ever happened in my life.

"You mean it? I can ride this year? I don't have to go in the truck?"

"Settle down. Let's get on in the house before your mom throws our dinner out the door."

Preparations for the cattle drive were always a big deal. It was a yearly event that had long been a part of our family history. The summer pasture was a fair way off in the mountains. It was a long drive getting them there, because those old cows walked just about as slow as "molasses in January." The trip was hot and dusty, and the sun could be scorching and unforgiving.

Momma expressed some concern to Daddy because I was so fair-skinned. She worried about me being in the hot sun. Daddy bought me the biggest-brimmed straw hat he could find that would still fit my small head. We agreed that I would be better equipped if I were to wear a long-sleeved shirt. I still remember the shirt. It was flowered, orange and yellow, and had bright, shiny white snaps down the front, just like my daddy's shirts. I wore a blue bandana around my neck and new Wrangler jeans. I polished my boots to a spit shine and stuck a magpie feather in my hat. I was ready to go.

The big day arrived. We were up before dawn. Sleepy eyed, I climbed into the saddle on the back of my buddy and we were on our way.

Princey had been around cattle his entire life. They must have seemed odd creatures to him, but as soon as he realized that he and I had the upper hand and were responsible for steering them in the right direction, he got right down to business! He was a regular cow horse. A calf would take off out of the herd, and Daddy would cry out, "Get him, little one." I would gently turn a rein this way and that and Princey would obey. We were a team.

It was a long drive that day. I remember drinking all the water in my canteen long before Momma showed up with the stock truck. I was thirsty, hot, and tired by the time lunch break came around. I climbed down off my horse, and suddenly I felt very odd. I had the sense that I was an extremely short person. My legs felt like cooked noodles. It was the oddest sensation. I had never before ridden so long on horseback. I began to understand why those old cowboys' legs were so bowed!

Momma questioned whether or not I should get back on the trail. She knew that I was tired and it had already been a long day for me. I begged them to let me continue. So, with lunch over and my water canteen full, I climbed back in the saddle and was off. We drove the cattle to a holding corral that first night. It seemed like the "old girls" of the herd knew exactly what to do once they arrived.

The sun was fading into twilight as we loaded up the horses and headed for home. I slept all the way home. I was tired and sore; Daddy carried me to my bed and tucked me in. "See you in the morning, little one." I moaned as I rolled over, and I fell into a deep sleep.

The morning sun was hours from showing its presence in the sky when we hit the trail again. I was a trooper, stubborn and determined that I was going to finish the job I had started. Day two was harder than day one. My mouth was constantly dry, and I was fighting deer flies as they buzzed around Princey. The cows seemed to be slower, and the minutes turned into hours. My back ached, my legs hurt, and the cows smelled. But when Daddy rode up and asked me, "How's it goin' little one?" I smiled and told him I was fine. This was hard work, but I couldn't let my daddy down.

At one point even Princey was thinking that this was just about enough for one day. I leaned over the saddle horn, stroked his face and whispered in his ear, "Just a little bit further, and we'll be there."

It wasn't long before the landscape changed. The forest opened up to a meadow, and you could see for miles. The cows picked up the pace; they seemed to know they were almost home. Off in the distance I could see a white No Trespassing sign on the gate leading to our summer pasture. We were almost there! I could see the fishing hole and could smell the creek. "Princey, we're here! Isn't it beautiful?"

We fished that evening and cooked our little brook trout over the campfire. Momma sure knew how to cook 'em. After we ate, we cleaned up camp, doused the fire, and headed for home. I wanted to sit in the back with Daddy and Grandpa and the horses. We rode all the way home without speaking a word. But I saw in my daddy's eyes that he was very proud of my little steed and me.

HAPPY TRAILS

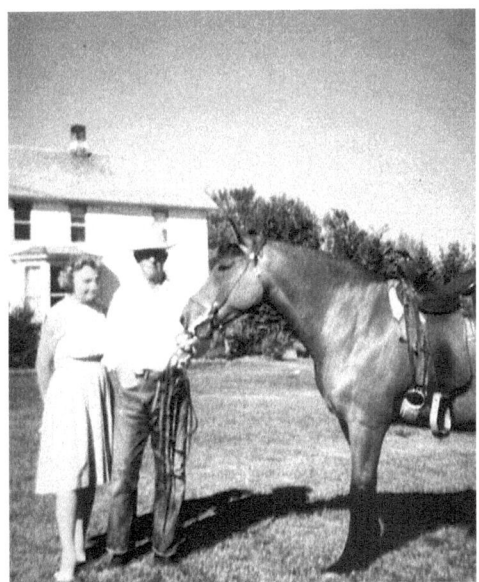

Photo of my Grandma and Grandpa Clark, Walter and Verna, on the Clark Ranch posing with Grandpa's horse, Monty

Photo of my dad, Ken Clark, on back of "Mr. Bud"

*Photo of me on my pony, "Princey," and my brother,
Phil on his little Shetland pony, "Bimbo."*

*Grandpa Walter Clark on "Monty," and my dad,
Ken Clark on his faithful horse, "Blondie," trailing
our Hereford cattle up to summer pasture*

Go, Granny, Go!

Several weeks had passed, and summer was in full swing. Grandma usually went to town several times a week to run various errands for Daddy and Grandpa Walt or just do what her "busybody" nature required. This particular week was different. In fact, my grandma had been home all week. She had been on edge too; something was definitely on her mind.

I was outside, helping my daddy with a few chores, when we heard the dinner bell ring. Quickly, we headed for the house. We had been working in the Quonset, so we had to walk past the shed where my grandma parked her car. The doors were usually open, even when the car was there. So, it seemed strange to Daddy that the doors were closed and barred. He stopped, turned to look, and made a clicking sound with his tongue as he moved the sprig of grass in his mouth from one corner to the other. An inquisitive look came over his face, and he dropped my hand. He turned to walk toward the shed and motioned for me to hurry on to the house to tell Momma he was coming. I ran ahead to wash up for supper.

It was several minutes before we saw Daddy came out of the shed. Momma, looking down the path from the kitchen window, watched as Daddy walked toward the house; he was laughing and shaking his head all the way. She met him at the kitchen door to find out the cause of his sniggering.

"Well, Lady," he said. "Mom tore the door right off her car! Darnedest thing I ever saw. The damn door is leanin' up against the wall. It's busted right off at the hinges, clean as a whistle!"

We all looked at each other as the dinner table broke out in laughter. It was no wonder Grandma hadn't been to town. How was she going to tell Grandpa Walt?

After supper, my daddy walked to Grandma's, knocked on the door, and asked her in a calm voice, "Somethin' wrong with your car, Mom? It's not like you to stay at home all week. Anything I can look at for you or check out for you?"

She stammered as the color drained from her face; she confessed her dilemma and begged him, "Can you fix it?"

"Well, Mom, I just don't think I have the know-how or the tools to do that. But I will drive it to town for ya." She pleaded with him not to speak a word of this to his dad.

Keeping his promise to not tell Grandpa, Daddy climbed in that car with no door and drove it to town. Of course, Grandpa Walt found out what had happened anyway. He was bound to find out. Everyone in town knew my grandma's car. Daddy told us that when he'd pulled it up to the shop, all the men had stood around with folded arms, surveying the damage and laughing. Verna had certainly outdone herself this time.

I think the car episode came after the time Grandma almost burned down the entire ranch. She was notorious for starting little piles of leaves and brush on fire and then walking away, leaving the fire unattended. One day, the wind was not in her favor, and the shelterbelt of trees started to blaze. She managed somehow to put out the fire all by herself, but not before it had done its damage and burned up several trees, shrubs, and garden hoses.

Months later, the trees still showed their scars. Grandma tried to convince questioning neighbors that the trees suffered from some sort of disease or blight. "Spider mites, I think," she said.

"Yeah!" Daddy joked. "They were infected with "Verna-itis.""

There's No Place like Home

I have so many memories of life on the farm. Precious recollections fill my life with smiles. But, in reflection, they weren't always happy times.

It was late in the summer of 1968. The hostility between my grandparents and my parents was growing more intense every day. There were arguments about money and all kinds of adult issues. I was only twelve years old, but I sensed that the storm that had been brewing was just about to commence.

When it happened, it was like a bolt of lightning that split our family down the middle. We were told we were moving. We were leaving the ranch. The feud had festered long enough; my daddy had painfully endured all he could. My grandparents had shut down Daddy's dream to someday own the ranch. In fact, when Daddy had asked to buy the ranch, Grandma and Grandpa Walt had actually laughed at him. They had told that him he couldn't afford it, that he would never be able to keep the ranch profitable, and that his crops would never amount to much. And then, when he said he was leaving, they'd mocked him, saying that he wouldn't be able to make it without them. "Oh, you'll be crawling back. It will just be a matter of time."

Needless to say, it was not an amicable split. It would be years before we would once again share holiday dinners with Grandma and Grandpa Walt.

Daddy and Momma wanted us to still love our grandparents, but the open wounds were pretty painful for them. I don't know all that happened, nor do I know all that was said. All I know is that my life was changed forever from that day forward. God had a plan for all of us, it seemed. I just couldn't see it. No longer would I swing on the corral gate or play in the loft or hear the clang of the bell beckoning us to come to supper. I would never climb the stairs to my bedroom again or ride my horse in the field by the river. What would my life be about? What would it be like? What was to become of my beloved home and my treasured apple tree?

The move from the ranch to the city was bittersweet. I had left behind my beloved home and my lifetime friends. I had said good-bye to my trusty companion Princey, and I had given my apple tree one last glance as we drove across the cattle guard. The smell of cow manure floated through the air as I watched the shelterbelt get smaller and smaller through the back window of the car. I couldn't understand why Grandma and Grandpa Walt hadn't even said good-bye to us the day we moved out.

My eyes were filled with tears as I thought of all of the wonderful things I would miss. Momma and Daddy were trying to be very positive, although their hearts were breaking too. They promised that things would be better and that our family would always stay together, no matter what.

Forty-four miles north, in Helena, our family took up residence in a new house—a brand-new house! I had my own bedroom, and my momma even let me pick out the color of the carpet and the paint for the walls. The walls were the color of lilac blossoms in spring, and the carpet was bright green, like freshly cut grass. The curtains were white and purple, and my bedspread was pink, my old one from the bedroom on the ranch. My room looked like a fancy dyed Easter egg! I had my own closet and a door to my own bedroom, one that closed and locked! I had never had carpet beneath my feet when I stepped out of bed in the mornings. This would be a treat! Better still, I wouldn't have to share a bedroom with my sisters!

As I remember, the winter of 1968–1969 was harsh. There was record snowfall and temperatures below zero that lasted for weeks. We felt safe in our new home, and day by day it began to feel more familiar and more comfortable to all of us. It was a small house when compared to the big old farmhouse we had left behind. Momma busied herself making curtains and arranging furniture until it was just perfect.

Springtime finally came, and my daddy geared up to plant trees and flowers and put in our lawn. To our neighbors, we must have looked like *The Beverly Hillbillies*. Daddy parked a real tractor in the backyard, and we all worked side by side, raking dirt and planting things. We built a fence and put in a driveway. None of the other neighbors worked as hard in their yards. I swear my daddy shamed them all into having the best-lookin' block in the neighborhood. It wasn't long before all our neighbors were painting and pruning and tidying up.

Sour Milk

Unlike many children growing up, I had the opportunity to know and develop memorable relationships with both my paternal and maternal grandparents. I have already spoken of Grandma and Grandpa Clark, but I must not neglect to tell you of Grandma Helen and Grandpa Stan Smith, my maternal grandparents.

In contrast to the temperament of Grandma Clark, Grandma Smith was perpetually kind and sweet, always looking for the good in people and in life's circumstances. Born April 11, 1912, Grandma Smith was long-legged, tall, and thin. Her face, like that of an angel, rarely wore a frown. Her graying hair was soft, falling gently around her face and neck. She had a mole under her chin that moved up and down when she spoke or chewed her food. I can remember sitting on her lap as a young child listening to her read me storybooks as I tipped my little head back and watched her "wart" wiggle. She smelled of clean, fresh soap and Jergen's lotion, and her hands were velvety soft and warm. She gave freely of her hugs and kisses. Children were all little angels, and life was beautiful, according to Grandma Smith.

Her house was cluttered with knick-knacks and framed photos of the family she dearly loved. Because of her glorious green thumb, she could plant anything, and it would grow; thus, her home was filled with plants of all shapes and sizes. She couldn't bear to throw away a plant, so if anyone had a sickly flower, they just brought it to my grandma, and she would nurse it back to health.

She was a great cook. I especially loved her date-filled cookies, molasses cookies, and sugar cookies. She proudly continued recipe traditions passed down from her mother and grandmother. When you arrived at my grandma's house, you could bet the tea kettle was on, or the coffeepot was brewing, and the lid to the cookie jar was off.

My memories of Grandpa Smith are of a gentle, loving grandpa who disguised himself as a feisty, cantankerous old man. Born June 16, 1907, he had endured some tough times with his family. He often looked for the faults in people, a way in which he could distance himself. He always seemed a very old man to me. He walked stooped over, and he wore a leather collar brace around his neck.

Years before, he had worked for the Northern Pacific Railroad and had been injured in an accident. Actually, he was lucky to even be alive. He had been doing some maintenance on the track and was in one of those small orange maintenance cars. At a crossing, a pickup truck had hit the car broadside, sending my grandpa and the car flying. Grandpa had landed on a track rail, breaking his neck. With the train approaching, workers had had to move him off the tracks before the ambulance arrived.

According to the doctor, it was had not been a good thing to move him at such a crucial time. In addition to his broken neck, he had had a great deal of nerve damage and was almost minus an ear. He had been in intensive care for days. When my momma had gotten the call from Grandma that my grandpa had been hurt, she had been told that he was not expected to make it.

Momma said that after he returned home from the hospital, he had been somewhat different. He was short tempered and cranky to my sweet grandma, oftentimes saying mean comments to her. Most of the time she would ignore him, but when he got the best of her, she would turn and tell him, "Now, Stan, you don't mean that!" I know Grandpa Stan was probably in constant pain, and it must have been intolerable at times.

However, he wasn't always ornery. He had a fun and mischievous side to him too. He would giggle as he sang his own renditions of a familiar tune or when he made up words to old-time nursery rhymes. Here's an example: "Old Miss Muffet sat on her tuffet, eating her curds and whey. Along came a spider, and sat down beside her, and said, 'Is this seat taken?'"

He would smile as a *heh, heh, heh* came from deep within his belly. We kids would fill the air with laughter in response to his clever creations.

Grandma would smile and say, "Stan, that's not how it goes. You don't want those little kids saying that one, do you?"

He'd just wink and continue.

Grandpa Smith loved animals too. He was always mending some bird with a broken wing or taking care of some sickly creature. You see, he really had a kind heart, but he didn't want anyone to know that he was really just an old softy under that leathery skin.

Once, I recall, Grandpa Smith and Daddy went out to shoot the foxes that were eating our chickens. They shot the female, not knowing that she had a den of young. When they found out, Grandpa felt horrible and couldn't bear to kill the babies, so he took them to his home and built pens for them. He took care of them until they were big enough and strong enough to make it on their own, and then he set them free.

For most of his life, Grandpa was a chain smoker, smoking unfiltered cigarettes. He coughed every morning, and I can recall that when I spent the night at their house, I would cover my head with the pillow so I didn't have to listen to that. He always slept on the sofa and had laid claim to his special chair at the table too. It was pretty much forbidden that anyone else sit in either place. And if you did sit in his chair, he would stand there and stare at you until you got the hint and moved.

In my earlier childhood days, Grandma and Grandpa Smith lived in Toston, Montana, in a railroad section house that smelled of bleach and kerosene. It was sparsely furnished but neat and tidy. We would often walk to Grandma's after school, where she would meet us at the door with fresh milk and warm cookies.

She loved to listen to stories about our days at school. She would let us read or color in her coloring books until Momma or Daddy arrived to pick us up. When she kissed us good-bye, her soft hands would cradle our little chins as she lifted our faces and gently kissed us on the forehead.

It was always very special when we were fortunate enough to spend the night at Grandma and Grandpa Smith's house. They loved us so much. They spoiled us with their affection and their attention. We never fell short of receiving love or attention around them. Grandma would lie on the bed next to us and sing us songs until we fell fast asleep. She would wake us in the morning with smiles and kisses and breakfast.

It was a cool spring morning, not long after little brother Phil had been born. The three girls had spent the night at Grandma and Grandpa's house, in order to give my mom and dad a break. Morning arrived, bringing with it a fresh scent of Missouri River air. Dressed in our pajamas, we scooted to the table for breakfast. Our request had been cold cereal and toast. Grandma placed the boxes of cereal on the table so that we could choose our favorites. She patiently waited as we made our selections and filled our bowls.

With spoon in hand, we waited as she poured milk over our cereal. We bowed our heads for grace, and then it was time to eat. I took one bite of my cereal and gasped. Choking, I spit my mouthful back in the bowl.

Grandma looked puzzled as she said, "What's wrong? Did you take too big a bite?"

"No, Grandma," I answered. "My cereal's sour."

"What do you mean, it's sour?" she questioned.

"Grandma, I mean it's *icky!*" She walked to the table, grabbed a spoon, and took a bite of Pam's cereal.

"Tastes just fine to me," she said.

"Yeah, tastes fine to me too," commented both Pam and Deb.

"Well, mine must be rotten," I said.

"Nonsense," continued Grandma. "You got your cereal from the same box that Pam got hers."

I begged, "Grandma, please taste mine. It's really sour."

Grandma walked over to me. She took a big spoonful out of my bowl and put it in her mouth. We watched as her eyes grew big, and she sputtered as she spit the mouthful into the sink.

"Oh, angel," she shrieked. "The milk is curdled."

Well, I didn't know what that meant, but the look on Grandma's face told me that it wasn't good. That cereal was icky! She had finished a bottle of milk on my cereal and had opened a new one for Pam's and Deb's bowls. She felt horrible. I "milked" this story for years and so remember that look on Grandma's face—it was priceless.

Grandma was always up for having a spot of cinnamon tea. She would brew regular tea and then would drop cinnamon candies into the cup. It was wonderful. Even today, I love having a cup of cinnamon tea with my dear, sweet grandma.

After Grandpa's accident, they moved from the section house at Toston. I could never keep track of where they were living from one year to the next. Grandpa didn't like staying in any one place too long. He bought and sold more property than most of those real-estate tycoons ever thought about. Poor little Grandma never knew from one day to the next whether or not Grandpa was going to get the urge to move. She tried to hang on to some of her memories and collectibles, but even that was difficult. Grandpa wouldn't allow her to save much.

In spite of their quirks and relocation habits, it seemed they were just always there for us. I looked forward to spending time with them whenever I could. They were so special to me.

When One Door Closes

It was January 1969, and my first day at a new school was frightening. The school building was so big, and there were so many kids. Momma walked me into the school that morning. She held my hand as we talked to a very nice lady, with a comforting smile, at the front office. Momma bent over, kissed me, and said, "Have a wonderful day. You'll be all right, won't you?"

I nodded yes, and with a smile, I watched her walk away.

I followed the lady down a long hallway. The floors were shiny, and the air smelled of fresh, new paint. Class had already begun when she knocked on the classroom door. A pretty, dark-haired girl answered the door with a smile. The teacher greeted the nice lady and shook my hand. He smiled and motioned for me to enter the room. Strange faces starred at me as I walked to the front of the room. The teacher introduced me to the class and showed me to my seat.

A while later, a buzzer sounded, and everybody got up and walked out of the room. "Hey, where did everybody go?"

I soon learned that we changed classrooms with the bell. This was a big change from my little schoolhouse in Toston. The bell never rang there, except to signal recess, lunchtime, or the end of the school day. There I had shared my grade with only one other student, a boy. That's how it had been since first grade. He and I had been best friends, and he lived across the field from me.

Here, at my new school, there were so many in my class. There were twenty-two students in my room, and there were three rooms of sixth-grade students. How would I ever remember anyone's name? And there were girls the same age as I was. At lunchtime the girls sat on one side of the lunchroom, and the boys sat on the other side and *talked!* And if you were a girl, your best friend wasn't a boy! In Toston, during recess and lunchtime, we'd played cowboys and Indians down in the spring ditch, running and jumping through the thick brush. Here, you sat and gossiped with other girls and flirted with the boys. It was so different and strange and *wonderful!*

I took to my studies with excitement and enthusiasm. There was so much to learn and see! We had a real library, not just a few old books in the back of the classroom. We had an honest-to-goodness gymnasium, rather than a grassy area next to the old PTA building. There were globes and maps used for social studies, real music books, and a real stage for our concerts. There was even an office with a principal, vice principal, and secretaries. I loved my new school. I loved to learn. I made friends easily, and soon I looked forward to waking up each morning and going to school. With the passing of each new week, I thought less and less about my old school back home.

Because I had attended a small country school, I had been blessed with a real one-on-one teaching environment. My teachers in Toston had been wonderful and had taught me well. You see, even when I was little, I had listened to the lessons given to the older students. I was way ahead of these city kids. I excelled in my schoolwork, so my sixth-grade year was relatively easy for me. That was probably a good thing, since there was plenty going on at home to confuse me.

In addition to his new job in town, Daddy drove all the way to the ranch every morning to feed the cows for Grandma and Grandpa Walt. I don't know what kind of arrangement they had made with him, but I know that it was extremely painful for him to face it every day of every week. He seemed beaten down and depressed. He didn't speak of Grandma and Grandpa Walt much. And when he did, the tone in his voice would change. He was angry and deeply hurt.

One evening, we were all seated around the dinner table when Daddy proceeded to make an announcement. Momma would be getting a job. It wasn't what they wanted, but it was an issue they had discussed at length. They really didn't give us a reason, but it was clear to see that the decision to put Momma to work was a painful one for all of us, especially Momma. She had done things before to help bring in money, and she had volunteered to work during elections and such, but she had never really worked outside of our home. She was scared, but she put on a happy face for us, and we all agreed that we would pitch in to make it an easy transition. I never realized how very painful the change would be.

Momma working outside our home caused a shift in responsibility for most of the domestic chores. Deb, Pam, and I quickly assumed the role of supper cooks, and many of our evenings and Saturday mornings were spent with housework. Daddy was never very good at housekeeping chores, but even he had to step up to the plate and help out. Momma was frustrated and tired when she got home each night from work. Her once-spotless house gave way to disorganization and a not-so-perfect environment. She didn't handle it well. We weren't used to her being irritable, and we were slow to accept coming home to an empty home after school; we became latchkey kids. The realization of "that was then and this is now," slapped me in the face each and every time I turned the key in the lock and opened the door to a silent house.

Daddy felt guilty about Momma having to work outside the home. They didn't argue about it, but I could tell it bothered him. He lived for the weekends, when things would sort of return to normal. Momma only worked Monday through Friday, and even though Daddy drove to the ranch in the mornings, he was home long before we stirred from our beds. We still had breakfast together before Daddy went off to his job, Momma went to hers, and we went off to school. We spent our Saturdays and Sundays doing family things. It was always a thrill to go for a Sunday drive after church or visit with relatives.

Daddy was usually the designated Sunday driver, and my momma was the tour guide-elect. We would often pack a picnic lunch and head for places we had never been. Daddy was notorious for getting us lost. In this category he fit the stereotypical male to a T. He would never ask for directions, and using a map for guidance—well, that was just not his way. Our Sunday drives frequently turned into adventures—long ones, indeed!

I'm Sorry

My parents were gifted in the art of listening. They very seldom fell into that trap of being caught off guard by their children. They listened, took mental note of what was going on, and then usually discussed the issue between the two of them. We had a pretty difficult time pulling the wool over their eyes.

Daddy was funny in the listening department too! He made quick and easy judgments as to whether or not he was qualified to listen to and give advice on a certain subject, especially female questions. After asking a question, we would look for a sign from him. If his eyes sparkled and his face lit up, we were in for a long, calculated explanation based on "dad-isms." If he began to sweat and furrow his forehead, we knew the answer would be "Go ask your mother." As we progressed into our teen years the questions became more serious, and there were a lot of the "go ask your mother" responses.

Moving to town seemed to necessitate a new way of thinking for our family and, most definitely, a new way of listening for my mom and dad. It became very apparent to me that living in town was truly different. Our new surroundings and our new-fashioned lifestyle demanded dramatic changes. Mom's focus was fragmented, and Dad concentrated on trying to make everyone happy. He listened to his family with the hope that he would clearly see what direction we should follow.

The art of forgiveness is not always easy, but it is simple. Daddy had perfected the art of listening and had turned his ear to his family. It was dramatically clear to him that his children needed their grandma and grandpa in their lives. Mom had petitioned my dad to make amends with his folks. In fact, I think it was Mom who facilitated us making that first trip to see them after our move.

I'm not sure if Grandma and Grandpa ever said the words "I'm sorry." But I do know that my dad did. It was several years before our relationship with my grandparents would once again flourish, but just having a second chance was a blessing.

Grandma and Grandpa sold the ranch in early 1970 and built a new house in Townsend, which was about eleven miles north of the old place. They had made some drastic changes in their lives as well. Our first visit to see them since the family split was most memorable.

It had been well over a year since we had seen them. After church, we drove to Townsend to share a Sunday afternoon dinner with them. As we were driving up to their home, I saw Grandpa peering out the window. He looked wonderful. A smile lit up his face when he saw us. He met us at the back door to the house. He had developed a little bit of a grandpa tummy, but his eyes were clear and his smile was warm and welcoming.

Opening the door he exclaimed, "Well, lookie here!" We filed in the door as he ushered us into their home. Once in the house, I could smell the ham baking in the oven. There was also the lingering aroma of freshly baked dinner rolls and homemade apple and cherry pies.

Grandma busied herself in the kitchen. It was comforting to see her in her starched dress. As I hugged her, that familiar smell of her perfume penetrated my memories. She wiped her hands on her apron and beckoned to each one of us. She looked us up and down as we greeted her. She pretty much ignored my mom and dad and focused on us. She threw out comments like "My, how tall you are!" and "My, how skinny (or fat) you are!" or "My, how grown-up you have become!" Her eyes twinkled as she listened to our tales of city life and what we had been doing in school. She pinched our cheeks and patted our rears and scooted us into the living room.

The surroundings were strangely unfamiliar to all of us. Grandma had obviously been shopping and had acquired all new furnishings, all except the dining room table and chairs. They even had a new color television. The house was larger than their home had been at the ranch. This one seemed the perfect size for a grandma and a grandpa. Their yard was well manicured, a by-product of their years of ranching and farming.

Surprisingly enough, the afternoon went well. We had a wonderful visit with them. It had been time to patch things up. I will be ever grateful to my mom and dad for having the wisdom and courage to teach and practice the art of forgiving. Deb, Pam, Phil, and I had many wonderful years with Grandma and Grandpa Clark. Our relationship with them would change and mature over the years to come. We shared so many good times with them. Some were still stressful, but then, that's life. Grandma mellowed with age but never really changed. Grandpa became delightful in his retirement years, trading his distant coldness for warm, attentive affection. His grandchildren and then great-grandchildren warmed his lap for years to come. His hand and heart reached out to his son, my father.

In their own way, my grandma and grandpa did regret the way they had treated my mom and dad. They just never quite knew how to say it. The years passed, and they grew to actually love and respect my mom. Mom was good to both of them as they grew old. She always remained at my dad's side, but she, too, softened with respect to my grandparents. And all it took was a listening ear and an "I'm sorry."

Young Love

Even though we had moved from the ranch to Helena, my sisters, Deb and Pam, maintained close relationships with some of their friends from the small town of Townsend, only a forty-minute drive south of Helena.

When I first met their friend Danny Herbst, he had already graduated from high school; he was six years older than I. He and his best friend, Craig Biggs, were sweet on my sisters and began spending quite a bit of time hanging around our house in Helena. Sure, my sisters loved them, but it seemed more like big-brother love to me, and eventually the boys resigned themselves to that fact.

Danny and Craig were best buds, like two peas in a pod. What one didn't think of the other one would. They shadowed each other. It seemed that every Friday and Saturday night they wound up at our kitchen table, persuading my mom and dad to engage in a friendly game of pinochle. Deb and Pam were sometimes not even at home during these visits from the boys. They would take off with their other friends or their boyfriends. But Danny and Craig would stay to play cards. They were champions at this game.

My parents would break out the snacks and the sodas, the leaf would be removed from the table, and the cry would be, "Let the games begin."

Daddy and Momma were the cutest pinochle partners you could ever imagine. They used little signals during the bidding process, thinking they were being so crafty. Danny and Craig would most always win. Relentless in their pursuit of being the champions, they were conscious of my parents' little schemes.

There was always laughter, and entertaining stories would be bouncing around the table. I had never played, but I thoroughly enjoyed pulling up a chair and watching and listening. I was eager to learn the game, and I remember Danny always answered my questions. He had such a way of explaining the strategy of the game and how it worked. He would often let me help him play a hand or two, calling me his "little partner." That made me feel special, because I so idolized my older sisters and their friends.

They would play this silly game way into the wee hours of the morning. Deb and Pam would return from their night out to find a rousing game still in progress. They would say good night, go to bed, and be fast asleep before the game finally ended. I tried to stay up as late as my mom and dad would allow. I sometimes got sent to bed early, but on certain nights they would let me remain at the table, and I would take it all in.

When the game was finally over and the snacks long gone, there would be hugs and good-byes at the door, along with blessings from Mom and Dad for a safe drive home. Danny and Craig would both walk down the sidewalk and wave at us before climbing into the car, packing with them another fearless pinochle victory.

Being the kid sister wasn't all that bad. Deb and Pam were really good about including me in their activities. They took me to movies and to the A&W for root beer. In the summertime, they would even let me tag along with them and their friends when they went to the lake. We would go swimming and play on the sandy beach, eat disgusting greasy potato chips, and drink soda until our bellies ached. My sisters and their friends would talk about girl things, like boys, hairdos, and makeup. Danny and Craig would play catch or Frisbee and kick sand on the girls. Sometimes they would chase the girls, and when they caught them, into the water they would go. I remember thinking, "I wish they would chase me and throw me in the water." But they didn't. When we had our fill of fun and sunshine, we'd head for home. We would climb into the car with wet swimsuits and sand stuck to our legs and tennis shoes.

It happened one late August weekend in 1971. School was about to start. We were all trying to get that last hurrah in before it commenced. I was going into the eighth grade. At age thirteen, I thought I was doomed. All the boys my age acted so stupid and immature. Their big goal was to see who could fart the loudest or who could spit the farthest. In addition to their lack of fine etiquette, they were all of shorter stature than I was.

I welcomed being with Danny and Craig. They were cool. They could drive a car with one hand on the steering wheel, window down, while resting the other arm on the door. They had heavenly eight-track tapes, and they even let me sometimes pick out the music. We would cruise down the road with The Grass Roots blaring *The River is Wide* from the tape deck, the wind blowing our hair. And both Danny and Craig were taller than I was.

It had been a great summer. I had spent a lot of time at home, babysitting my little brother. But weekends had been reserved for fun at the lake, or the park, or just downtown with my friends. It was an incredibly warm August day, and with school just around the corner, a day at "Senior Beach" was just what my sisters wanted.

Danny and Craig showed up at the house about ten o'clock in the morning. I remember walking out of the bathroom with a towel on my head. Craig slapped at the towel. "Hey, little sis! Are you coming? We're going to the lake."

My eyes went directly to Deb and then to Mom. Both seemed to be saying that it was okay. I said, "Sure. When are you taking off?"

Danny piped up— "Right now! We're going to the grocery store, and then we're heading out."

"Well, I just got out of the shower. I need to dry my hair."

"We said the lake. You know, water and swimming— get it? Why would you need to dry your hair?" Danny questioned.

Craig stepped in and said, "Okay, we'll go to the store with Deb and Pam. You get ready and we'll come back for you. But you better be ready!"

Away they went to the store, and into the bathroom I scurried. While I was drying my hair and primping, Momma was spouting, "Don't forget to use suntan lotion." (There was no such thing as sunscreen at that time.) "Remember, you burn really bad."

"I'll remember, Momma."

Be it known: my entire family and all my friends agreed that if all my freckles would just grow together, I would have one bona fide tan. But that will never happen!

The horn honked, and out the door I went. Gary Pucket and the Union Gap, a groovy group, were screaming from the radio as I climbed into the back seat. We waved at my mom, and off we drove to the lake—and to a life-changing afternoon.

When we arrived at the lake, I grabbed my towel, my bag, and a six-pack of Coke, and I headed down to the beach. Deb, Pam, Danny, and Craig carried everything else to a picnic table not far from where I had spread out my towel.

I had my swimsuit under my cutoffs and T-shirt. Not wanting to take off my clothes in front of everybody, I went up the hill to the little brown hut they called a restroom. Earlier that summer I had bought this really cool lime green-and-white, gingham-checked two-piece suit. It had ruffles on the top and was pretty skimpy, according to Dad. I loved it!

Picture this: a skinny little redhead, with white skin, huge freckles, and a lime-green swimsuit. I was a fox! But I had noticed something: I was beginning to fill out a little. The ruffles even made my insignificant breasts look larger than they really were. I stood admiring my reflection in the piece of tin tacked to the wall of the hut. My breasts were actually not much larger than medium-sized mosquito bites, but at least they were finally noticeable.

I wrapped a towel around my waist, grabbed my clothes, and down the hill I went. The boys had already been in the water by then and were sitting on the picnic table sipping cold sodas.

I haven't described the boys yet, have I? Dreamy—that's what they were. Dreamy! Craig Biggs was charming with that little-boy grin. His brown hair was straight-combed to one side. His eyes were light blue, and they twinkled with every mischievous thought. He wasn't extremely tall but had a well-proportioned body. He wore cutoffs all summer long, and I must say, those tan legs were mighty choice.

And Danny Herbst? Oh, Danny was so fine! He had the most unforgettable hazel eyes. They were kind, sincere eyes. Even though it seemed to have mind of its own, his gorgeous, wavy, brown hair always looked amazing. And his contagious giggle was his calling card. He was taller than Craig was and slenderer. He had the sleek profile of a runner, with lean legs and a notable butt. (Sorry, he just did!) He had finely tuned back and chest muscles and well-defined muscles in his arms. Like I said, he was dreamy. In my opinion, Danny was the epitome of a Greek god.

Flipping my hair back in the breeze, down the hill I came in my lime-green glory. Craig caught a glimpse of me out of the corner of his eye. With an impish grin, he motioned to Danny with his head.

In a single moment I was being carried to the water, kicking and screaming all the way. They were going to throw me in! Wow! They were throwing *me* in the water. This was so cool! I yelled and sputtered and gasped for air, but deep down inside I felt special! I was finally one of the "girls," with breasts and everything!

The rest of the afternoon I sat in the shade next to the table, reading, watching and listening, and applying suntan lotion. I was, however, uncomfortable with the lingering stares from Danny. I looked up from my book several times to check out the scenery, and we would exchange a smile or two, but I didn't know what to make of his gaze. The day was so peaceful.

When it was time to go home, we packed everything into the car. But when I started to get in the back seat, where I always sat, Danny said, "Why don't you sit up front, in the middle, with Craig and me?"

"Me? In the front? With you? Really?"

Craig agreed. "Sure, then we can put the cooler between Deb and Pam. That would be a good place for it."

Good plan! The mystery was that there was nothing left in the cooler, and there was plenty of room in the trunk, where it had always been placed before on *every* other trip to the lake.

"Okay," I said. I climbed in the middle, next to Danny at the wheel, and Craig climbed in next to me. Now, this was a little Ford Falcon, not exactly the roomiest car in the world. Things were pretty tight up there, so we had to get pretty close. Anyway, we turned onto the highway and headed back to Helena. Danny's hand slowly dropped from the steering wheel to the outside of my knee. "Okay," I said to myself. "This isn't intentional. This isn't what I think it is—or is it? No, it can't be; I am just imagining things. Okay, my leg is touching his leg, like, you know, skin to skin. His hand is on my knee, I think! *Jeepers!* Is anyone else seeing this?"

Craig was turned talking to Deb and Pam in the back seat. My heart was beating so fast that I thought it was going to jump out of my chest. I didn't hear a word of their conversation. All I could hear was my heart pounding in my ears! My knees began to shake, and my stomach was feeling queasy. Danny's hand moved from the outside of my knee to rest lightly on my thigh! That voice inside my head screamed, "Oh, my gosh! Does he know what he is doing? I can't breathe!" His hand touching my thigh made my entire body shiver! Oh God, what was happening?

I was quiet all the way home, concentrating on the feeling of his touch, and wondering. Danny only moved his hand once in a while, in order to shift or put in another eight-track tape. Then, ever so gently, his hand would return to rest on my thigh. It may not sound like much, but after I had been thrown in the water and gotten to sit in the front seat of his car, this boy's touch catapulted me into a new way of thinking. In my mind, I *had* grown up in the course of one afternoon. Danny was flirting with me! It was glorious!

P.S, I Love You

School started, and I found myself wrapped up in my schoolwork and my friends. I usually walked to school in the mornings and then home again in the afternoons. Our house wasn't far from the school, and I did enjoy the time to myself. Home was always a little crazy, with my sisters and my brother around. Mom didn't get home until after five thirty, and Dad sometimes didn't get home until close to six o'clock. As a rule, dinner was the responsibility of the kids. Mom always had a plan for us after school. This involved cooking and cleaning and laundry. Then it was dinner, dishes, homework, and bedtime. Once in a while, we would indulge in a television show or two, but most of the time we just wanted to hole up in our rooms with the radio on, reading or doing homework.

It was an amazingly pleasant Wednesday afternoon, and the walk home from school was nice. Like typical kids, my best friend and I had kicked a rock all the way to school that morning. Surprisingly enough, we found the same rock and kicked it all the way home. Standing by our mailbox, I waved good-bye to my friend. I pulled down the door to the mailbox and grabbed the few pieces of mail from inside. As

I walked up the sidewalk, I shuffled through the envelopes. Then my books slipped from my hands to the walk below. My heart raced and my skin tingled.

There in my hand was a letter addressed to me. It had no return address on it, but it was in Danny's handwriting. I'd have recognized his writing anywhere. I had sat next to him many a night as he wrote everyone's names on the score sheet while playing cards. I slowly turned my back to the front door. My finger slipped beneath the envelope flap as I lowered myself to sit on the step. I pulled from that envelope a letter that began, "Dearest Becky, I don't know how to tell you this, but I believe I must. I know I am much older than you, but I need you to know that I think I am in love with you." I looked up in disbelief. I turned to see who might be looking, and then I stared down at the letter again.

Could this be real? I read the first two sentences over and over before I read on. "I want to spend every minute I can with you. No one has ever made me feel like this before. I know that this sounds crazy, but I think about you all of the time. I don't want to scare you away, and I don't know how this will ever work, but I needed to tell you." The letter went on to say that he knew that my parents would not understand right now but that he would be satisfied just to see me, as always. He said that it would be special just to be near me.

Well, I read that letter repeatedly, probably fifty times or more. With each reading, a new sensation would envelop me. I was scared and excited and everything in between. Was *I* in love? Was *he* really in love with me? What was love, anyway? How had this happened? What would happen next? How would I act when I saw him again? Oh no! He and Craig were coming to visit Friday night. What would I say? What should I say? Who could I tell? What would Daddy say?

I hid the letter. I kept it from everyone. I didn't even tell my sisters or my best friend. I didn't know what to make of it. I certainly didn't have any idea how to handle it. I wasn't anything special to look at. I was thirteen, for gosh sakes! I was actually pretty plain looking. I dreamed of being a raven-haired beauty like my mother, but instead I was fair-skinned and redheaded like my dad. I had big brown eyes and freckles on my nose. I wasn't too short or too tall. I may have been a little on the skinny side, and I was somewhat of a tomboy. But I had noticed that hips were beginning to appear and my chest was developing. Oh yeah, as if a tomboy who looks like Little Orphan Annie has a chance with the Greek god from Broadwater County! What could he possibly see in me?

The next two days were hell. I was a nervous wreck. Every time I closed the door to my bedroom, my hands would reach for Danny's letter. My stomach was in knots. I couldn't sleep and I couldn't focus. I had no idea how I would even act around him. What was I going to do?

Friday evening came. They would be here soon. What was I going to say to him about the letter? The doorbell rang. They were here.

"Beck!" Mom yelled from the kitchen. "Get the door. It's the kids."

I slowly opened the door and there, standing before me, were "the boys." Danny's smile was incredible. With raised eyebrows, he said, "Hello, can we come in?"

I stared, speechless for a moment, not knowing what to do or say. "Oh, Danny," I mumbled. "I'm sorry. Where are my manners? Of course you can come in. How are you?"

Craig pushed past us both. "Gonna stand here all night? Hi, Ma—feel like a card game?"

Danny's eyes met mine. Although it was only for a few seconds, it seemed like an eternity. Never before had I seen him in this way. I didn't even have to tell him. He knew I had received the letter. And my smile meant everything was okay. He grabbed my hand and squeezed it as he walked by me on his way to the kitchen to hug Mom.

Over the next few months, Danny and I became very close—in secret. Mom and Dad knew I cared for him, but they did not know the extent of our relationship or just how much I cared. We spent a great deal of time together. Most of the time it was with my family, but sometimes we were alone. Once in a while, he would pick me up from school and drive me home. But always, always, he was a perfect gentleman.

It was several weeks before he even held my hand. And I can tell you, *that alone* was an extraordinary experience! On that memorable occasion, his hand closed around mine, ever so softly, as his fingers stroked the top of my hand. I felt flushed, almost dizzy. "Gosh! What is happening to me?" I thought to myself. "This must be love! Only love could make a person feel this way."

We talked a great deal about life and family. He was very close to his parents. He came from a large family, but I could sense that he was close to his siblings. His mother was a gentle woman, with a smile as infectious as Danny's. His sisters were absolutely gorgeous, and his brother was a hunk, with an also-notable butt. I would often go to Townsend to visit my grandparents, and I always found time to slip over to see his mom, either at their family restaurant or at their home. I constantly felt welcomed, and I thoroughly enjoyed my time with his family.

My Soldier Boy

One special afternoon, Danny and I slipped away together, and he drove to the fairgrounds. After parking, he turned and looked at me with those beautiful, haunting eyes as he began to speak. "Beck, I have something I need to explain to you. Now, don't interrupt until I have finished. I have joined the army, and I leave for basic training soon, at Fort Lewis, in Washington."

My heart stopped. The conflict was raging in Vietnam. Our nation's young men were dying there—and I was not prepared for this. Tears welled up in my eyes. "Why are you doing this?" I questioned.

He quietly explained, "I feel I need to do this; I have to do this for many reasons."

"How long, Danny? What am I supposed to do without you?"

"Look, you are so young, and you need some time to just be a kid and grow up. Experience all you can, while you can. I'll come home. I promise. I've got you to come home to. Maybe someday we can have a real relationship, but right now you are just too young and too special for me to blow it. I need to do this."

I was devastated. The decision had already been made, and the reality of it all was looming in the very near future.

We spent a lot of time together before he left, many nights of playing cards, bowling, and going for long walks. There was lots of handholding, and we engaged in deep conversations about our future together. There was something that bothered me, though. Danny had never kissed me, well not on the lips anyway. He had given me pecks on my forehead and cheek, but I'm telling you, he was not like any boy I had ever met—or even heard about. He still treated me like a sister, and I was confused.

Somehow, my sister Deb sneaked me into the Marlow Movie Theater to see the feature movie *Romeo and Juliet*, starring Olivia Hussey. It was a controversial film, and I wasn't supposed to go. Dad would have killed Deb first and then me had he ever found out. The rating didn't allow admission to thirteen-year-olds. I did look and act older than I was, but not by much.

Danny and Craig met us there, and I sat next to Danny, in the dark, in the balcony. We held hands through the entire movie, and I reveled in the fact that I was with him. There was, however, one part in the movie that gave it its particular rating. In one scene, Juliet flashed her breast while reaching for her robe, and in another scene, Romeo stood for an instant with his bare-naked bottom exposed. Of course, this made me very uncomfortable. My palms became very sweaty, and I squirmed a little in my seat.

At that moment, Danny turned his head and smiled. I turned to gaze at him, as my upper lip began to quiver. Slowly, I slouched, and my head pressed against the back of the seat. He bent toward me, keeping his eyes fixed on mine. Closer, closer, closer …

"Now, we'll have none of that," whispered Craig as he slapped Danny on the shoulder. "Watch the movie—this is the best part!"

I could not believe it! I think Danny had *almost* kissed me.

The day of parting came much too soon. We all went to the bus depot to say good-bye to Danny. I remember crying so hard that I could barely see through the tears. I shall never forget the feeling of sadness that overwhelmed me. I whispered good-bye and held so tightly to him in an embrace I was sure my parents would question. I buried my face in his sweet smell, and as I closed my eyes, I prayed to God for his safety and his return home. It was one of the most emotional times in my life. I watched as my family said their good-byes. My dad even had tears as he shook Danny's hand and uttered, "Good luck, kid." My eyes burned and my heart ached as I watched him climb aboard that Greyhound. The door to the bus closed, and the engine revved as the bus pulled away, leaving the lingering smell of diesel in the air. Tears stung my face, and I watched as the bus turned and then drove out of sight. My soldier boy was off to the army.

I cried myself to sleep that night. In the dark and quiet of my room, I clutched his letter close to my heart and wept for the emptiness I now felt.

Every day I would quickly walk home from school to get the mail before anyone else could. I knew Danny would keep his promise to write to me as soon as he was able. It was several days before his letter came, but it did. It was a beautiful, but sad, letter. He briefly explained how things were going for him in boot camp. He said that it was hard but he was doing okay. He said he missed me and thought about me every day. His only request was that I write to him as often as I could.

I made a personal vow to write to him every day, so that he would know how much I cared and know that he had a special someone waiting for him at home. A little encouragement from home could only help and would hopefully make his time at Fort Lewis pass quickly. I carefully addressed each letter to Daniel Ray Herbst, Private, First Class, and then wrote his Social Security Number on the envelope. I thought I would never forget it, but it seems as though that number has escaped my memory, just now.

The weeks went by. I dove into my schoolwork and spent time with my friends, just being a teenager. However, I was the talk of the school. "Did you know? She has a boyfriend who's in the army. Isn't that cool! He is so much older than she is. Wow!"

Consequently, I did not show even the slightest interest in boys at school, or they in me. Why would they? How could they compete with my soldier boy? I was a mystery and somewhat of a complex individual to them.

Danny's leave was fast approaching. He would be home for a brief visit before he began his tour in Vietnam. I was terrified to see him, but I wanted to see him. I just didn't know if things had changed for us. It was clear that my feelings for him had grown stronger, and I had done some growing up too. We had corresponded each and every week. Sometimes his letters were very heartbreaking. He missed home, and he missed me. We had become so devoted to one another.

There were even times when he was able to call and talk on the phone. He tried to call when he knew I would be home alone, or at least my mom and dad would be gone. But on the nights that he miscalculated, Mom and Dad were thrilled to talk to him. In fact, the whole family would talk.

I couldn't say anything that was very intimate during those times, but he knew how I felt. My letters, however, were full of a young lover's passion. I spent many nights fantasizing about a future with Danny. My fantasies were enough to keep me content for now and enough to drive me just a little crazy.

Danny's homecoming had arrived. I can barely describe how I felt when I first laid eyes on him. He stepped down off the bus and turned to look at me. He was so handsome in his uniform! He carried himself differently, and his gait was surer. He had always been slim, but his stature had somehow changed. He stood so tall, and his wavy brown hair was short, accenting his slender chin. He was gorgeous. And that smile! Oh, that had not changed. He could reel me in with that smile. I ran to him and he picked me up and squeezed me ever so hard, holding me in his arms for the longest time. My heart pounded and my lips whispered, "Welcome home." He was home! My soldier boy was home!

I had a difficult time sharing Danny with his family, but he needed to be with them. I knew that. But his leave time was so short, and I knew that the pain of saying goodbye was just around the corner. I wanted to spend every minute I could with him. This was the first time that my parents showed some concern about my relationship with Danny. Things were noticeably different between us. They considered him part of the family. He was like a son, but the age difference between him and me was a concern for them. After all, I was their little girl.

One afternoon Daddy questioned me about my feelings for Danny. I was honest with my daddy and told him that I loved Danny. "Yes," he explained. "I do too." That was that! But his ever-so-watchful eye was on us.

Sixteen Candles

It was the week of my sixteenth birthday. My mom and dad had bowling league on Wednesday nights. Dan knew this. I remember begging my sister to let me go out for a short time with Danny. He and I were just going to go for a drive. I begged her, "Please, please, don't tell Mom or Dad! They wouldn't understand. They would get upset." Sister Pam agreed and gave me permission to go for a Coke.

It was March, so it wasn't very warm. Well, the saying in Montana for March is "In like a lion, *out* like a lion." That year held true.

I sat very close to him in the car, we held hands and, yes, I did the girl thing and cried, because I knew he would be gone in such a short time. He reassured me that it would all be okay.

We hadn't been gone long when he said, "I need to take you home and get back to Townsend. Mom is expecting me home kind of early tonight."

"I understand," I muttered. "Walk me to the door?"

We walked around to the side of the house, where cement stairs led up to the back door. He said, "Sit with me for a minute?"

"Sure, but it's kinda cold out here, Danny."

We sat, side by side. With his arm around me, I heard him whisper, "Becky, may I kiss you?" My heart was beating so fast that I couldn't answer. I couldn't even look at him, and as I looked away, shivering in the cold, he scooted closer. He reached in front of me, and his hand cupped my chin ever so gently, pulling me toward him and lifting my face upward to gaze into his eyes. Our eyes locked, and he smiled and then pressed his lips to mine. My eyes closed as our lips melted together. His mouth was soft, and the warmth of his kiss moved through my body like a spreading wildfire. His arms surrounded me, pulling me to him. In that moment, that very moment, I surrendered.

I will *never* forget that kiss. It was my first kiss. It was beautiful and simply perfect. My butt was frozen to the cement, but I was on fire. Folks say that your first kiss should be special, memorable, and sweet. Mine certainly was.

Danny's leave was short and saying good-bye to him this time was harder than even I could have imagined. At night I had horrible nightmares about Vietnam. I worried when I hadn't heard from Danny several weeks after his departure. I called his mom, who was also worried and who also had not heard from him. "If we find anything out, we'll call you," she reassured me. He finally called and told me what had happened.

They had been set to fly out of California to Vietnam. At the airport, Danny had been feeling faint and had left his group to go to the men's room. There he had been overcome by dizziness and nausea and had fainted. When he came to, he had found himself in an army hospital, where he had been diagnosed with meningitis. His group had shipped out, but he had remained back in California until he could recover. Danny had been so sick that he'd been unable to contact his family or me. I wanted him home! Damn the war! Damn the army!

I always thanked the good Lord for his love and protection. God was so good! Danny had taken typing in high school; when he arrived in Vietnam there was a position as a clerk, and he fit the bill. He was still in harm's way, but I now felt more certain that he would come home—home to me. My belief in God's mercy kept my heart still. I continually wrote to Danny, telling him in each and every letter that I loved him. He returned my letters, every one of them.

My relationship with Danny had been an accelerated-growth adventure. I had experienced an incredible, unbelievable relationship with a true man. Danny was kind and had a sense of humor that warmed my heart. We were so close, yet we had not had a sexual experience, which was certainly fine with me. I wanted to share that with him, but I wasn't anywhere near ready to take that step.

One night, during his second leave from the army, we drove to The Limestones, a favorite place for young lovers in a small Montana town. It was a moonlit night, and Danny pulled off the road, parked the car, and turned off the motor.

That night, Danny was anxious, looking at me in a different sort of way. Our conversation was warm and comfortable, and it wasn't long before we began to kiss. Gently caressing me, his hand innocently touched my breast.

Danny pushed himself away from me and sat upright, saying, "I can't be here with you right now. I have to take you back to your grandma's—now! This isn't right. I shouldn't be doing this." Staring straight ahead, he continued, "Your daddy will string me up by my thumbs, or worse, if I ever hurt you."

I didn't understand. He *wasn't* hurting me. It had been wonderful. I was feeling as I had never felt before. I longed for his tender kisses and warm embrace! What did he mean, hurting me? I moved closer to him and whispered, "But you're not hurting me, Danny. It feels incredible." He was trembling, and beads of perspiration were popping out on his forehead. As he turned to look at me, tears welled in his eyes. I closed my eyes and placed my head in my hands. Oh, dear God! I was so naïve. My poor, sweet love! How could I be so stupid? No, Danny was right! This *was not* a good idea.

Our relationship had become so intimate, yet no one would have believed that this young man never pushed me to do anything inappropriate that night. He was a perfect gentleman. We drove to Grandma's in silence as I lay my head on his shoulder. He kissed me sweetly and said, "I love you." As I walked down the sidewalk, I turned to wave goodbye, but all I saw were the taillights of his car. With every passing day, I knew more deeply that he was my one true love.

Danny's experiences in Vietnam left some deep physical and emotional scars that changed him forever. He saw more pain and suffering than I could imagine. He coped with life in a different place, a war-torn country. I just couldn't identify with anything he was experiencing. He was fighting a war in a location far from home, thinking about a young sweetheart he had left behind. Meanwhile, I was in Montana, being a kid. He had grown up, and we had grown apart.

He wrote letters expressing concern about making it home alive and seeing his family again. His letters were filled with a longing for the old days and with plans for his future. My letters from home spoke of things that were happening in my day-to-day life. I wrote to him about cheerleading, ponytails, history tests, and movies. I told him I thought maybe I should date other boys and just be a teenager for a while. To him, that was the dreaded "Dear John letter". He was hurt and angry. I still wrote to him, but his letters to me became fewer and farther between.

Danny Herbst did return from Vietnam at the end of his tour, and I was very happy to see him, although he appeared somewhat detached. I don't know much about his experiences during the war. He was relatively guarded when speaking about them. Loud noises, such as airplanes going over and cars backfiring, alarmed him, and he was on edge. He was unsettled and anxious to leave Montana almost as soon as he came home. He was so distant.

He said he wanted me in his life always, but he let me know how devastated he had been when he'd received that letter. He questioned how I could do that to him. Dear God, I was only a kid. I was thinking about high school and graduation and college. I had plans for my life. It wasn't easy to be so young and have a boyfriend six years older than I was and away in Vietnam. We kept in touch some after his return, but I don't think that he ever forgave me.

I Wear My Sunglasses at Night

With the sound of the bell, the halls filled with students. Frenzied, we all scurried about as we raced to our next class. With my books clutched against my chest, I walked quietly, with my head bowed. I was not having a good day. A bump from behind made me turn as someone brushed by my arm. Quickly turning forward, I managed a small grin as he turned and quickly said, "Sorry." And then, in an instant, he disappeared up the stairs.

I had never seen him before that day. It was my junior year in high school. I knew pretty much everybody in school, and I was certain this kid was new. I questioned my girlfriend in my third-period class. She said she wasn't quite sure what his name was. She did, however, know that he had just moved there from Great Falls. He was supposedly this great athlete, and rumor had it that he had been in trouble with the law.

It was lunch hour, and the school emptied as students poured out the doors. The grass in the front of the school became a sea of laughing teenagers as they sat devouring their lunches in the warm sun. I sat leaning against the brick building, enjoying the sunshine and the company of my friends.

I saw him again, and I watched as he slowly walked alone down the front sidewalk, heading for the parking lot. His face was expressionless, his stride unbroken. It was as though he didn't notice the heads turning to watch him. A hush fell on the gathering of students; all eyes were on the stranger. I guessed he was about six feet in height. His shoulders were broad, wide even, in comparison to our football coach. He was statuesque; the muscles in his legs rippled with each step, and his arms swung with determination and purpose at his sides. He had bright, curly red hair, and his eyes were a piercing blue. His sharp facial features were softened only by a sprinkle of freckles. He hadn't smiled just now, but I recalled our encounter earlier that morning and remembered how he had looked at me. He was mysterious. He weaved through the parked cars and vanished.

Shielding my eyes from the sun, I searched the horizon. Chatter soon replaced the quiet, and I watched as an unfamiliar car sped down the dusty road toward town.

In the crowd I heard someone talking about the stranger, and I cocked my head to listen. News was that he had just transferred to our school from Great Falls High School. He was a star defensive football player and accomplished in track and field. His dad was a clergyman, and he lived right next to Hill Park in the Episcopal rectory. Supposedly he was engaged to marry, and I once again heard the rumor of a bout with legal authorities.

The bell sounded to indicate that lunch was over, and we returned to the confines of school. I sat daydreaming, not really listening at all to my world-history teacher. When he called on me, the class laughed as I stuttered and stammered before asking the teacher to please repeat the question. That was how the rest of my day progressed.

That evening at dinner, I mentioned to my mom and dad that there was a new kid in school. I told them how mysterious he was and that I was sure he was the biggest guy in our high school. "What's his name?" Mom inquired.

"Neil, I think. His dad's a minister, or at least that's what kids were saying. I heard he got arrested for something back in Great Falls too. I wonder what he did."

"Well, before you go about thinkin' certain things about someone, you should learn the truth, don't you suppose?" Dad interjected.

"Yeah, I know. He's kinda cute. He has red hair and freckles, Daddy, just like you!" We laughed as we continued on with our chitchat about the day.

Over the next several weeks, I learned a little more about the stranger. His name was, in fact, Neil Campbell. He had not been arrested. It had simply been a case of mistaken identity. He had looked like someone the law was after and had been taken in for questioning. He wasn't engaged, although he did have a girlfriend, and she was older than he was. We had had occasion to bump into each other in the halls, and he had managed to smile and say hi. From afar I observed this mystery man, never imagining what would happen in my senior year.

Sweet September

The summer before my last year in high school was a lot of fun. I was a cheerleader and spent a great deal of time with the other girls in the squad as we prepared for football season. There were trips to the lake and outings with my family; there were movies and evenings out with friends. I was still trying to get over my relationship with Danny. I did have a lot of friends that were boys, but I was pretty leery of the going-steady thing. I was just having fun being a kid. I had my driver's license, and my mom and dad let me use the car as often as I wished.

My sister Debbie was married and lived in Denver, Colorado. Pam was also married and lived in Pendroy, Montana. So, it was just Phil and me at home. I remembered all of the times my sisters had carted me around with them, so I did try to include my little brother in my fun. He wasn't much trouble, and Mom appreciated me keeping an eye on him.

I was so excited that I didn't sleep a wink before the first day of school. I wanted to see all of my friends and was anxious to get my senior year under way. With plans to go to college, I knew that getting through this year would bring me closer to my goal. I had slimmed down an extra few pounds, and I had some cool new threads. I felt pretty good about myself going into my senior year.

We had won our first football game in our home stadium. It was exhilarating! The fall had been magnificent in all the golden splendor of the turning leaves, and the air was crisp with excitement. I was laughing as my friends and I jumped with glee and headed onto the field to congratulate our players. I was shocked, however, when the handsome stranger picked me up and whirled me around in a victory spin. It was Neil. He put me down and grinned before turning to run past the cheering fans. I smiled and watched him bound away, curious when he stopped to turn and look back at me before disappearing into the crowd.

My hands were in dishwater when the phone rang. I yelled, "Mom, can you get that? Dad? ... Phil? ... Anybody?" There was silence as I dried my hands and reached for the phone. The phone cradled on my shoulder, I said, "Hello. Who? Oh, hi. Uh-huh. Sure. That would be fine. Yes. Great, I'll see you then. Okay, good-bye."

I hung up the receiver and turned to see my mom as she came toward me. "Who was that on the phone?" she questioned.

"Neil Campbell, that new boy from school. He asked me on a date, next weekend, after the Libby game. Is it okay?"

Mom, although shocked that I was so matter-of-fact, was relieved that I was finally going on a date, because she knew I was still hurting over Danny. She grinned as she said, "Yes, of course. It should be fun."

"Mom, I've heard that this Neil has a really hot temper. I sure hope we don't lose the game."

"Oh, well, somebody has to lose. It's just a game."

"Right," I said.

Monday at school, I saw Neil several times in the halls. He stopped outside the library and asked me if he could carry my books to my next class. I hesitated and then agreed as I piled them in his arms. We walked together, not sure what to say to one another. He smiled and asked if I had plans for lunch.

I responded with a "No, not really."

"I'll meet you in front of the school. I packed a lunch for both of us. We'll go for a walk, okay?"

"Sure, that sounds okay," I said. He said bye as I walked into my classroom. Stepping back toward the door, I peeked around the corner only to see him disappear from sight as he bolted up the stairs. As I sat down in my desk, I began to wonder why this guy was constantly appearing out of nowhere and then vanishing just as quickly. He was a puzzle, and I was committed to putting the pieces together.

I waited for him outside the school, watching as the students filed through the doors. I spied his hair as he moved from the shadows. He walked toward me with a sheepish grin. We strolled into the sunshine around the back of the school, and I was surprised when he motioned for me to climb the fence surrounding the graveyard. It was an old Catholic cemetery that had been there for years, long before the school was even built.

"It's okay," he said. "I do it all the time. It's quiet, and nobody bothers ya, especially not the people in here." I laughed as I took his hand. Carefully balancing on one leg, I climbed over the fence. It was peaceful. The trees towered over us as leaves floated down to rest on the tilted and crumbling tombstones. He brushed off a headstone and directed me to sit. I obliged, and he sat next to me, cross-legged on the moist grass. We sat in the stillness and shared lunch. He talked a mile a minute, only stopping to take another bite of sandwich. I listened intently as he spoke of his family.

His mother and father had divorced when he was quite young. His real dad lived back in Great Falls and was a traveling salesman, with a Scottish temper and a love for sports. His mother had remarried an Episcopalian priest, which was what had brought them to Helena. He had two younger brothers, both redheads, and also two cats. His stepdad had a dog, and he had not two, but three grandmas, and one grandpa. His mother was a teacher who worked in a sheltered workshop.

I told him a little about myself and my family, but our conversation was cut short with the ringing of the bell.

Tuesday and Wednesday were much like Monday had been. We spent lunchtime together in the cemetery. Neil was quite attentive, and we were beginning to feel a little more relaxed around each other. Wednesday, after school, I walked to the practice field and sat in the bleachers to watch the football team prepare for the upcoming game.

I was amazed at the ability of my newfound friend. He was physically aggressive and an incredibly intelligent ball player. He read each and every play and was always there one or two seconds before the offense was ready for him. The other players rallied around him as he chanted encouraging words to his teammates. He was quick to temper if he made an error and charged on, giving more and more of himself. He was a powerhouse, full of passion for the game.

The coach, recognizing his capabilities, played him both on defense and offense. He was our star middle linebacker and ran first string offensive fullback. He was also on special teams. He rarely tired! The coach would have to be persistent in his demand that Neil sit out a play before he would yield. Then, pacing back and forth on the sidelines, he would shake his head, eager to get back into the game.

I thought I might catch his eye as I sat watching practice that afternoon. However, seeing him practice, I knew that he was oblivious to me. Others had gathered in the bleachers, but he was unaware of all.

Looking down, I spotted a couple as they made their way up the steps of the stands. The gentleman was holding the woman's hand, sort of pulling her along. The woman was mesmerized by the action of the play, and the man tugged gently at her arm. He was a tall man; she was much shorter than he. He had on a bright-red coat and a stylish black hat. She was wearing a camel-colored wool coat and a beige knit cap.

Still entranced by the goings-on, the woman removed her cap and ran her fingers through her short red hair. I had never seen these people before, but that red hair was a dead giveaway. They had to be Neil's folks. Stepping down the bleachers, I stopped and turned to look at the couple. I caught the attention of the gentleman, and he smiled as I approached.

I put out my hand as I said, "You must be Neil's parents? My name is Becky."

His mother's trance was broken as she turned to me with a huge smile. "Oh, you must be the cheerleader my son told me about. It's nice to finally meet you. This is Jimmy, and my name is E. V. Reevie—well, it is Eve."

Eve was stunning. She was small in stature, but I sensed that this little lady was not to be messed with. She had an infectious laugh, and the more she talked the higher the pitch of her voice became. She had gorgeous blue eyes and sharp features. Neil had told me that his grandfather was Jewish, hence the characteristic nose. She had a little-girl grin and full, pouty lips.

Jim Reeves was extremely handsome. He was a tall man with the kindest eyes I had ever seen. His skin was dark, and his hair was beautiful, turning silver gray. He had an unbelievable smile and appeared very confident. He was most cordial, in an English-aristocratic manner. From beneath his red coat, I spied the collar of a clergyman.

We talked for a bit and then I bade them good-bye. Dinner was my responsibility tonight, and I knew I had better be heading for home. Jim and Eve wished me luck in the upcoming game, and Eve shouted, "We'll see you again soon?"

I smiled and waved, and as I walked to my car, the team ran by me. I turned to smile and say hi, but Neil stormed by without even a glance in my direction. I shrugged my shoulders, saying to myself, "Well, maybe he didn't see me." I climbed into my car and headed for home.

The next day at school, I waited for Neil between morning classes, as usual. He never showed. Once I caught a glimpse of him, but he was gone before I could speak. At lunch he was very quiet. I talked a little, but my words solicited little response, giving me a very uneasy feeling. Even the cemetery seemed to give me the shivers. I couldn't put my finger on it, but I felt like Neil was hundreds of miles away. I asked him if we were still going out on Saturday night. He answered yes, but then he quickly retreated to God knows where.

I waited for him after school, only to see his car as he drove away. I stood there, perplexed, wondering if I had done something wrong. Had I said something that had offended him? I was certain that I hadn't done anything. I turned on my heel and headed back into the school for cheerleading practice.

BACKING THE BRUINS—The Capital High cheerleaders will make their first home appearance of the season Friday afternoon when the Bruins meet Billings Senior in a Class AA Eastern Division football game at Vigilante Stadium. The cheerleaders for 1974-75 are, left to right, Judy Sangray, junior; Colleen Sanders, cheer queen April DeVore and Becky Clark, all seniors, and Jody Stromberg, junior. (Staff Photo by Gene Fischer)

Photo of my Varsity Cheerleading Squad

Photo of Neil Stuart Campbell, Football

Winning Is Everything

The Libby game was horrible. First of all, it might as well have been in Siberia. Libby, Montana, was almost three hundred miles from Helena, and the bus ride was uncomfortable. We gathered at the school parking lot before dawn. The team bus idled in the dark, and I looked for Neil as the players boarded the bus. He walked slowly, head down as he climbed the steps. I yelled, "Neil, good luck!" He didn't even acknowledge my presence.

As I said, the game was awful, in more ways than one. It was bad enough that we lost to Libby, but the way we lost was heartbreaking. There was less than one minute left in the game. Our team was ahead by five points, and Libby had the ball on their own fifteen-yard line. They needed a touchdown to win. They had had a good running game and only needed inches for the first down. It was fourth down with one yard to go. The snap occurred, and the quarterback stopped, faked, and stepped back for a pass. Neil, reading the play, bowled over the offensive line and sacked the quarterback. The crowd roared, and we took possession of the ball on Libby's fifteen-yard line.

Our defense had held them. They had been within inches. The home crowd moaned as our offense took the field. The coach signaled for Neil to stay there, and the players took position.

It was just supposed to be a series of plays to run out the clock. I don't know who called the play, but after the first snap, the ball was handed off to Neil. Carrying the ball as fullback, he ran, but he was hit from behind, and the ball fell from his grip.

Libby recovered the fumble, and with the next play, they went in for the touchdown. We were stunned. We had lost the game by one lousy point. This was not a good thing, especially if you were going out the *very* next night, for the *very* first time, with the *very* guy who had fumbled the ball, giving the other team the *very* opportunity they needed to win the *very* lousy game! I was doomed!

"Great!" I groaned. "This is just perfect. Why don't I just get a gun and shoot myself!"

I crumpled to the bench as the team slowly and quietly shuffled by. The clicking of their cleats in the dusty track made a pitiful sound. They were somber. My eyes met their looks of defeat as I watched the players pass.

Neil, helmet in hand, glared at me with a cold, gray stare as he pushed his way to the front of the procession. Quickening his step, he walked right by me without uttering a word. The other cheerleaders looked at each other, not quite knowing what to say to me.

The bus ride home was quiet. There wasn't a whole lot to celebrate. Everyone else soon fell asleep, but I couldn't. I was sick to my stomach with the smell of diesel fumes, but I couldn't forget the way Neil had glared at me. It left me with a sickening feeling.

I was terrified just thinking about our date the next night. What would I talk to him about? I had never been around anyone as intense as this kid was. He was like a walking time bomb, ready to explode. "Am I ready for this?" I thought to myself. "Well, maybe he'll call off our date. Yeah, I'll bet he does. Dear God, I hope he does."

My dad picked me up from the school, and as we drove home, he said, "Sorry about the game, honey. It was a tough loss."

"Yes, it was, Daddy. I'll tell you about it tomorrow. I'm really tired."

It was almost noon when Mom opened the door to my bedroom and asked, "You gonna sleep all day, or are you going to get up?"

"Do I have a choice?" I asked.

"No, not really. Get your little butt out of bed. Oh, and by the way, Neil called. He'll pick you up at six thirty."

I grabbed my pillow and pulled it over my head, wanting the world to just go away.

"Mom, what am I gonna wear tonight? The brown sweater or the striped one? Whadda ya think?"

"Well, sweetheart," she said, "I don't really know. I like them both. You pick."

"Mom, you're not really being much help," I whined. "Oh, Mom, by the way … don't mention the game to Neil. He was super upset last night, and I don't think he will want to talk about it at all. Please, just say hello and nothing else, okay? Oh, and don't refer to last night's loss with that *just-a-game* phrase. I don't think he would understand. Okay, Mom?"

"Sure, sure," she said. Good—at least we were clear on that.

Six thirty arrived, six forty-five, and then seven o'clock. "Where is he?" I grumbled. "We're going to miss the start of the movie. Great! Not only is he a football madman, he's late too."

I heard the car drive up, and as the doorbell rang, I ran for the bathroom. "Mom, can you get the door? I'll be just a minute. I just want to make sure my hair looks okay. Pleeeeeeeeease!" I closed the bathroom door behind me.

Leaning against the door, I looked over my shoulder at my reflection in the mirror. I had chosen the striped sweater. It had bright multi-colored stripes, and it hugged my curves. I liked the way it looked on me with my tan corduroy suit. I had straightened my long red hair and parted it down the middle. I had put just enough makeup on to cover up the redness of my windburned cheeks from the night before. My lips were chapped but glistened with a soft color of lipstick. I bent straight over and stood up quickly, flipping my hair back to give it fullness. I grabbed the hair spray and spritzed it one last time. "Well, Beck, this is as good as it's gonna get."

I had opened the bathroom door and turned to walk down the hall, when I heard my mom talking in the living room. "Oh, my Lord, what is she saying? She's in there with him, *alone*!" I came around the corner only to see my mother, who had been given *very* specific instructions, bent over and peeking around Neil's arms as he sat with his head in his hands. The words coming out of her mouth were unbelievable, frightening—and brave!

"Neil, it's only a game. You'll win the next one."

"*Mom!*" I shrieked. And in one complete breath I spouted, "I see you've met Neil. Dad, this is Neil Campbell. Neil, don't we have to go? We're already late, and we don't want to miss the movie. I won't be home late, guys. Bye!" And out the door we scurried.

What a disaster! What was Mom thinking? Did she have a death wish? How could she do this to me?

You could have heard a mosquito sneeze in the car on the way to the movie theater. There was absolutely no conversation at all. Neil pulled his car into the parking spot and turned off the car. Starring straight ahead, I said, "I'm sorry about my mom. She was just tryin' to make you feel better. She didn't mean anything by it. She's really a nice lady, you know. She doesn't understand that the game means everything to you. Please don't be upset."

Pausing for a moment, he said, "Hey, that's okay. Let's go see a movie." And with that, he opened his door. I sat there for a few seconds, shaking my head. Reaching for the door handle, I was startled when Neil opened my door. He offered his hand to help me out of the car and then closed the door behind me.

Our first date fell together quite nicely. First of all, he took me to see the epic movie, *Doctor Zhivago*. Then we went out to eat late-night Chinese food. After leaving the restaurant, he drove up McDonald Pass, west of Helena, and parked the car in the forest. We went for a walk, talking all the while. It was getting late, and I suggested that we get back to the car. I was cold in my lightweight coat, and I knew that my mom and dad expected me home on time.

He kissed me once under the moonlight, opened the car door for me, and said, "Let's get you home." He was charming.

Time in a Bottle

What began as a mysterious friendship soon evolved into a meaningful relationship. We were inseparable. I shall never forget the first time Neil invited me to dinner at his house. One day after school, he told me that his mother was fixing meatloaf and that he and his family wanted me to join them for dinner. Although I had met his mom and stepfather, I really didn't know them, nor had I met his brothers. Jokingly, Neil said, "Dinner is at six o'clock, and I won't take no for an answer."

I was nervous, and I arrived at his house about ten minutes early. He lived in the rectory right next door to the Episcopal Church. It was a regal two-story brick house, positioned between the church and a city park. Walking up the sidewalk to the front door, I clenched my fists at my sides, not knowing what to expect. I rang the doorbell and nervously fidgeted as I waited for a response. Jim, his stepfather, answered the door, greeting me with a warm smile, and said that Neil and his mother were in the kitchen. Neil was helping Eve prepare dinner. Jim escorted me into the living room and then excused himself to check on how things were progressing in the kitchen.

Their home was enchanting, filled with unique collections of artifacts and statues from places all around the world. They also had some gorgeous antiques, and I found myself looking around the room in awe of the wonderful things on display. Jim returned, and I began asking questions about the origin of certain pieces. They were fascinating! Jim, I learned, had traveled extensively throughout the world and had been employed in several interesting fields prior to the ministry, including the CIA during The Bay of Pigs invasion of 1961.

Neil soon joined us in the living room and announced that dinner was almost ready. I was impressed with the interaction between him and Jim. Neil politely motioned for us to follow him to the dining room. What lay before me was magnificent. The table was formally set with the most beautiful china I had ever seen. The Blue Willowware pattern was dramatically set against orange table linen. Everything was so elegant. I wondered if these people ate this way every night.

Eve was a delightful woman with an incredible flair. She was a talented artist, with an uncommon knack for decorating. She possessed a unique knowledge of furniture and antiques, and she was an incredibly creative cook. The meatloaf did not even remotely resemble any meatloaf I had ever tasted. Not intending to be rude in any way, I inquired about her ingredients. I never knew anyone actually cooked with eggplant, but Eve Reeves did! It was peculiar but extremely tasty! We even enjoyed a small glass of wine during dinner, something unheard of at my house.

The dinner conversation was stimulating. They were so interested in my life on the ranch and asked me all kinds of questions about my family. They were delighted to talk about their family as well. Our dialogue was effortless, and I instantly felt at ease in their presence. It was as though I had known them my entire life.

Neil's brothers were typical younger siblings, snickering to each other and teasing Neil. They did, in fact, also have red hair, although the color was not nearly as intense as Neil's was. There we were, all seated around the dinner table, all with red hair—except, of course, for Jim. I had never been in such close proximity to this number of redheads at one time. It was a bizarre occurrence, I'm sure. Strangely enough, I felt as if I belonged.

So many things happened during my senior year of high school. There was cheerleading, which took up an immense amount of time. Neil and I were most definitely the most talked-about couple in our school. It was like a fairytale. I came to know and love his parents. His family became my second family, and my family became his. I found it difficult to get used to his up-and-down moods, but I began to accept the fact that he was just a very intense individual.

During the week of a football game the routine was pretty much standard. On Monday and Tuesday, he would be fine, walk me to my classes, eat lunch with me, and we would spend part of our evenings together. On Wednesday and Thursday, he would become more distant, wouldn't walk me to classes, would still eat lunch with me but hardly speak, and we would rarely spend any part of these evenings together. On Friday, I would be totally ignored. He wouldn't even look at me in the halls. His focus would be on the upcoming game, and I could have fallen off the face of the earth for all he knew. If we lost the game, I wouldn't hear from him until he was good and ready—maybe not even until the following Monday. If we won the game, we would have a great night out.

He was so hard on himself. It seemed that there was so much pent-up frustration and energy in him. We talked about so many things, but I really couldn't understand or relate to where he was coming from when he spoke of his parents' divorce. Thank God I had never experienced that. I also couldn't comprehend the fact that he only saw his dad once in a while. He wanted a relationship with his father, but it was difficult to maintain one because his dad lived in another town.

Neil had a strong faith in the Lord. He was also very sensitive. He seemed to understand women and the complexities therein more than any other young man of his age. He wrote some of the most poignant poetry I had ever read. He even wrote verses just for me. He was a good artist too. I was amazed at how creative and fluid his paintings were. He definitely had a soft side. This was quite a contrast to the hard-hitting football player he was.

He was always late, never on time. His fifteen minutes would turn into hours. We had a hard time ever planning anything for a date, because we were always running behind. This was an area of continual argument between us. I couldn't stand being late for anything. Neil made me late for school. He often brought me home late from dates. He was even late for Sunday Services and he lived right next door to the church! The only thing he wasn't late for was football practice. He was *always* there early.

Like Father, Like Son

From the time of our very first date, Neil made plans for me to meet his father. It was apparent that this was very important to him. He spoke highly of his father, but I sensed that there was a distance between them that was torturous for Neil. Several times, after Neil had painstakingly made arrangements for us to meet, his father canceled. Finally, one evening after a football game, we were invited to join his father at a dinner club. We walked into the restaurant and were immediately greeted by several of Neil's father's friends. Neil seemed very nervous and anxious to find his father's table and sit down. We followed the sound of the laughter and within minutes were seated at the table with this animated group.

Murdo, Neil's father, was charming, like Neil. He wasn't what I had expected. I don't really know what I'd expected. He was quite handsome and had a quick wit. The jokes were flying around the table—until someone mentioned the night's football game.

Although I thought Neil had played a good football game, Neil didn't want to talk about it to Murdo or the others seated at the table. He was very uncomfortable when his father brought up the score and the stats. It was clear that Neil felt as though he had to be perfect in his father's eyes. His performance in that evening's game had been good; however, Neil felt it had been flawed, and he felt shame. I sat very quietly, not really knowing what to say.

Neil was very sweet. He tried to make me feel welcome and bring me into the conversation. I found it nearly hopeless to fit in with this group of men. They were all drinking and telling jokes and being very loud. Murdo, however, was most attentive to his son and me, and told us to order anything that we wanted off the menu! Neil sat quietly as we waited for our meals. We engaged in short conversations with several men at the table. Unfortunately, the conversations usually wound up centering on the football game.

One of Murdo's friends sensed that Neil was very uncomfortable and soon directed his conversation to me. Quite frankly, I don't think he found cheerleading and ranching to be interesting subjects, but I appreciated the shift in the focus of the conversation. And I suddenly began to feel more at ease.

The evening soon came to an end. By the time Neil and I left the restaurant, I understood a little more about the complex relationship that he had with his father. He wanted to be a part of his father's life, and he so much wanted his father to accept him for who he was, not for what he could be. Over the next several years, I watched as their relationship took twists and turns. It would appear strong one day, and the next day it would come crashing down around them.

Murdo Campbell was a complex individual, talented in many areas of his life. He was one of four sons born to "Duff" and Elizabeth Campbell. All four of the boys were star athletes in their hometown of Great Falls, Montana, and all four of them succeeded in the football program at the University of Montana. They were all well-recognized and were the pride of their parents and the Great Falls community. Talent in the area of football was just like breathing for young Murdo Campbell. He was sure of himself and was a team leader. He met, fell in love with, and married Neil's mother, Eve, in 1956. They, like Neil and I, became inseparable. And they, like Neil and I, had had some very difficult obstacles to overcome in their relationship.

I remember once questioning Murdo about that period in his life. He didn't have much to say, and I was certain that our conversations from then on would not include reminiscing old times. I concluded that the breakup for Murdo and Eve must have been horrible for all concerned—and especially horrid for Neil. He loved both of his parents, and he loved his stepfather too. There was a dark cloud over his head whenever he spoke of the divorce. I couldn't even imagine how terrible that must have been for him and his brothers. Neil somehow had assumed the role as head of the household at a very young age—an accelerated transition from youth to adulthood.

It was clear that Murdo loved Neil and that he wished the very best for his son. He did, however, expect perfection in the game of football. The prize for near perfection would be in the form of a football scholarship to the University of Montana. It was evident that Neil's future and college plans would most definitely have to include football and the University of Montana. Why, it was Campbell tradition, and no son of Murdo's was going to break family tradition!

Beauty Queen

In early September, Labor Day weekend marked a very special time of year. Not only was it the last long weekend of summer, but I cherished the night of *the* televised event of the season, live from Atlantic City, New Jersey. Every year I sat glued to the television as the top finalists competed for the coveted title of Miss America. As a young girl, I would visualize myself walking down a lighted runway, adorned with a crown, as Bert Parks sang that all-too-familiar song, "There She Is." I would smile, tears of happiness streaming down my face, and take a bow, while the crowd roared with excitement as they stood in ovation. I would say to myself, "One day I *will* be Miss America."

As I grew older, I surveyed the contestants as they paraded in their stunning evening gowns, and I hung on their every word as they addressed the audience. I was also their toughest critic in the talent competition. Between my mom and dad and me, we always picked the winner. With my pen and tally sheets in hand, nothing came between me and the Miss America Pageant.

I recall the very first time I ever saw the show in color. Grandma and Grandpa Smith had a new color TV, and they invited us to their house to watch the pageant. It was the most breathtaking pageant ever. The evening dresses were gorgeous in full color, and the talent costumes were exquisite. I was confident that someday I could enter a pageant and vie for the coveted crown of Miss America.

It was the winter of my senior year. Still dating Neil, I was relieved that football was over and basketball season was underway. Between cheerleading, choir, church activities, friends, schoolwork, and Neil, I was one very busy teenager. One afternoon, the guidance counselor stopped me in the hallway and said that she wanted to discuss something with me after school. She stated that several other girls would be attending a meeting regarding participating in a scholarship pageant, and she wanted to know if I was interested. Now, as I said, I had been infatuated with this pageant stuff since I was a little girl. I was so ecstatic to think that I was considered worthy to attend such a meeting. I remember I called Mom on the phone to ask her if I could stay at the school and attend. She was busy at work and couldn't talk long, but she said that I could stay if I went home right after it was over. For the remainder of the day, I was somewhere in the clouds and all I could think about was that stupid meeting.

The gathering was in the auditorium. Exactly five minutes before it was to start, I walked through the doors, only to be bombarded by an auditorium full of teenage girls, all talking and all wanting to be Miss America! There were dozens of girls, and I felt that most of them were much prettier and more popular than I was. I took a seat in the back and listened to the presentation from the stage. All those interested in competing were encouraged to pick up an application following the meeting. The forms needed to be completed and turned in the following Monday. A long line of girls quickly congregated and began moving slowly to the front of the auditorium to pick up their applications. There were so many! I knew most of the girls that had stayed behind and were now standing in line. There was a lot of beauty and talent here, but I figured I might as well pick up a form, just to see what it was all about.

I left the auditorium feeling somewhat melancholy, and I walked out of the school. I had discussed with Neil the fact that I was going to attend this thing after school. He had taken my car and *promised* that he would return to pick me up. Twenty minutes or so passed, and still no Neil. It was so cold out. I had promised Mom that I would go straight home, so I started for home on foot. I remember walking against the freezing wind and thinking all the time, "Could I really do this? Could I be Miss America?" I wasn't even thinking of how mad I was at Neil for being late to pick me up.

At the dinner table that night, I told Mom and Dad about the meeting. My brother joked about it, but my mom and dad were very supportive. They were always so encouraging. Their advice was to give it all I could. Mom was so convincing when she said, "You have as good a chance as any other girl in school. I think you should do it. You've always wanted to do this kind of thing. This is a good opportunity."

We looked the application over, and both my mom and dad told me that they would help me with it on the weekend. Mom took me to her office and helped me type the application, so it looked very professional. I was anxious for Monday to come. I turned in my application form early on Monday morning. Hoping that there wouldn't be very many turned in, I asked the counselor how many she had received. She answered, "Lots!" She explained that the pageant committee was looking for approximately five or six interested girls. "Seventeen applications have been turned in. I think we may have to have an elimination round!" My heart sank. What, pray tell, was the bloomin' fascination with this pageant thing, anyway?

The announcement came on Wednesday. There would be a preliminary competition. The pageant committee would be choosing three girls from my high school. Only three out of seventeen! I was so nervous! Who wouldn't be? The competition would be the following Saturday. It would consist of an interview portion and a talent segment. I found a suitable piece to sing, and my mom coached me with some interview tips. Basically, these were: "Sit up straight, don't chew gum, look them in the eye, be polite and—above all—smile. Oh, and keep your knees together!" Well, I was ready to go, or so I thought.

To compete in a pageant had been my dream for many years. I wanted so much for that dream to become reality. I was intrigued with the entire Miss America Scholarship Program. There were valuable monies awarded, and it was an incredible opportunity for a young woman to get a start on financing a college or university education. This elimination round was a pretty big hurdle to get over. I needed to be in the top three to participate in the Miss Helena Pageant. Could I do it?

Saturday came almost too fast. The program was a bit confusing and somewhat disorganized. I tried to focus on the task at hand, but I honestly felt uncomfortable with the whole idea of competing. It just seemed like such a small percentage of us would even get the chance to move on. It didn't seem fair. My family and friends were there to support me. Mom and Dad and Jim and Eve wouldn't have missed it for the world. Neil, on the other hand, was so nervous for me that he was dreadfully uncomfortable. I was scared, but I tried not to show it.

My interview portion went very well. It was more like visiting with friends, not really a stuffy interview at all. The judges were just real people who had been around the pageant program for a long time. The talent portion was the most nerve-racking part, but at the same time, it was exciting. I loved to sing and had been singing since I was very small, but even I was amazed at how well I did. I had practiced in front of a mirror at home, using a can of deodorant for a microphone. I wanted to appear relaxed and confident. My objective was to make the audience and the judges believe that I did this sort of thing all of the time.

When I stepped out on the stage, I picked a focal point at the back of the auditorium, just above the heads of all those people in the theater. Mom had given me some good advice. She had said, "Just picture everyone sitting in their underwear." Believe it or not, it worked. My voice only cracked once, in the beginning. So, even though I was scared, I didn't show it. I might add that the pageant director looked very funny in his underwear!

At the conclusion of the afternoon, we all waited in our seats for the winners to be announced. Silently, I kept saying over and over, "I did my very best, and I'm perfectly all right with that." But I also offered up a fairly self-seeking prayer, which surprised me, because that was not generally my nature. When my name was called as a winner, I cried. Since I'd been a little girl, I had waited for this moment to come, and now it had arrived! I was on my way! Atlantic City, here I come!

Am I Ready?

Practices for the Miss Helena Pageant were held in the basement of a local church. They took place two or three nights each and every week. I was being pulled in a hundred different directions! I don't think that Neil quite understood my busy calendar. He felt neglected, and when I tried to explain to him that this was as important to me as football was to him, he would try to understand. I really believe that he wanted me to do my best. He just didn't want me to forget about him. Neil tried to be supportive. He really did. But the thought of his girlfriend prancing around in a swimsuit in front of hundreds of people wasn't his idea of amusement. He wanted me to do my best, but I wondered: did he want me to win?

Mom and Dad were awesome. They were my best supporters and my foremost critics. They were so encouraging, while being totally honest and sincere. They kept reinforcing the fact that I could do anything I made my mind up to do.

There were so many big and little things that I needed in order to prepare for the pageant. Mom worked in a downtown office, so every day on her lunch hour, she shopped. She was the consumer of the century, putting together the most incredible pageant wardrobe I had ever imagined. She made this task her number-one priority. First, I needed an evening gown and shoes.

Now, shopping in Helena, Montana, was somewhat different than shopping in New York City or Los Angeles. I wasn't sure what the difference was, but I was certain it had something to do with current fashion sense and choice selection. Montana was not noted for setting any major fashion trends, nor was it even celebrated for keeping up with the times. "Fashionologically" speaking, Montana was behind the rest of the free world by about five years.

I had no idea that my mother would even know where to begin to look for an evening gown. Much to my surprise, my mom knew about every shop in town. There was, in fact, this one little dress shop that was my mom's favorite. It was owned and attended to by a couple of little old ladies. If my memory serves me correctly, The Mary Moore Shop was the fulfilling delight of two sisters with divine tastes for fashion. They were highly selective in their inventory. Each dress in their shop had to be a one-of-a-kind creation, and all were of incredibly high-quality fabrics and timeless styles.

Mom had been shopping on her lunch hour earlier in the week and had found what she believed was the perfect dress for me. We waited for the weekend to arrive so I could accompany Mom downtown to see the Moore sisters and the dress.

The little bell tinkled as we opened the heavy wooden door to the shop. The smell of rose sachet filled my nostrils as the door closed behind me. The shop appeared empty, except for the colorful gowns gracing the cubicles that were placed around the room. From behind a velvet curtain peered a little face with the kindest eyes I had ever seen. "Oh, I see you've brought your sweet daughter to look at that gem of a dress. Sister dear, Mrs. Clark is here with her young pageant hopeful. Can you bring out the dress?" From one sister to another, their kind comments were spun into threads of soft and generous conversation. They made me truly feel like a queen. It was an afternoon I shall never forget, and the dress—oh, the dress!

It was as turquoise blue as the waters of the Caribbean and as graceful as a waterfall cascading down a mountainside. The dress was the most beautiful garment I had ever seen! The skirt was chiffon, full and flowing, and the bodice was of a shimmering knit. The long sleeves and mandarin neckline gave the dress interesting charm and society flare. There was no doubt that this dress had been designed and created just for me. To this day, I don't even know how much it cost. That was something my mom never discussed with me, but I know it was expensive.

The Moore sisters laughed with sheer delight to have matched such a fine dress with a young woman such as myself. They said I would be the talk of the town, and they promised to be in the audience to see me take the stage in my heavenly gown.

I needed an interview dress too. Again, Mom performed her shopping miracle and found just the perfect dress for me. It was simple and elegant. I rented a swimsuit from the state pageant headquarters, so I didn't have to buy one. It was a one-piece, hot pink suit. I have no idea what made me choose the pink one. Truthfully, I think I just wanted to finally wear pink, a color I had stayed away from since the whole scene in the grain bin. I just thought it would be fun to wear a color that was generally taboo for redheads.

Choosing just the right piece to sing was not an easy task. I was a true alto, with a strong voice. My choral director was certainly helpful in determining what song would be appropriate but also diverse enough to show the quality of my voice. True love songs are timeless, and the song "I Honestly Love You" by the Australian artist Olivia Newton John was a popular love song of the decade. The words were simple and beautiful, and I truly believed that I could do the song justice. I wanted to feel the song I would be singing, and I sensed that this selection would enable me to express myself. One of my friends from school offered to accompany me on the piano. We practiced every day until we both felt comfortable with the music.

A great deal of time and effort went into preparing for the Miss Helena Pageant. There were rehearsals and style shows, photo shoots and interviews. All of the contestants were given support and help from the committee, but I was fortunate to have the help of my family and my friends.

I met so many wonderful girls in that competition. Most of them were older college girls. They seemed so much more sophisticated than I and certainly knew so much more about themselves than I did. I learned from this experience, discovering so many things about myself. I learned my strengths and weaknesses. I tried to fill my days with positive affirmations. Over the weeks, I determined that no one accomplishes anything in life without effort and conviction. It may have seemed like a ridiculous competition to some, but it was the greatest endeavor in my life so far.

February 22, 1975

The Miss Helena Pageant was considered one of the biggest social events of the year for our small community. The auditorium was filled to capacity with people; it was standing room only. There was a bustle of excitement in the air as the Miss America overture bellowed from the sound system. Backstage were fourteen young women with butterflies in their stomachs and dreams in their hearts. Some had become good friends during the weeks of practices. They had watched each other grow and change and had encouraged each other to strive for their personal best.

I was one of the youngest contestants in the pageant that year, and when the music started, my eyes searched the dressing room from girl to girl. I wondered who would be the crowned queen. I was competing against some amazingly talented individuals. In my heart, I wanted to be victorious and wear the crown and the title of Miss Helena, but I honestly felt as though I were a winner already. I believe that this experience was tremendous and was one of the first steps in discovering who and what I really wanted to be in my life.

February 22, 1975

I wish that I could describe that night, so that everyone could experience it just as I did. It was unlike anything I had ever imagined. I was frightened, nervous, anxious—even petrified—but my fears were calmed with moments of confidence and gratitude. I was grateful that I had so many people who loved and supported me. I don't know what my parents actually thought of the entire process, but they told me that I could do it, and that meant a great deal. I recall my mom and dad saying that no matter what the outcome, they were proud of me. Those words rang in my head each and every time I walked out on that stage.

Luckily, the bright overhead lights almost blinded me, and I couldn't see much past the first couple of rows. I could sense the audience but was uncertain as to how many people were actually there. Walking out on stage, I once again tried to focus above and behind the crowd, searching in the darkness for something that would keep my eyes fixed. I could faintly make out a little girl, all dressed up, with her little elbows leaning on the railing of the balcony. She seemed mesmerized, and her smile and attentive stare captured me. I watched her from the stage, remembering another little girl who had once dreamed of being Miss America.

The first competition, and the most difficult for all of the girls, including me, was the swimsuit competition. What were they thinking when they came up with this one? Okay, stay with me on this: parade around on stage, in the middle of winter, in a swimsuit, while wearing high heels. Make sense? We were all very glad when this portion of the pageant was over!

The talent competition was stiff. There were dancers, orators, a baton twirler, a pianist, a flautist, and several vocal performers. We had all practiced in front of one another, so we knew what to expect, but I had never seen the girls shine as brilliantly as they did that night. I was happy for all the girls as they stepped off the stage, having given it their very best. Somehow, I knew my performance tonight would be special as well.

I was contestant number ten. I walked out and stood center-stage behind the closed curtain as the piano was moved into position for my accompanist. One of the stage crew handed me the microphone, and I watched as my friend took her seat at the piano. Through the monitor, I could hear the emcee as she introduced me. Then it was my turn, and the crowd applauded as the curtains parted. A moment of silence came over the crowd, and I nodded my head, the cue for my friend to begin the intro. The tone from the piano was lovely, and I followed measure by measure, anticipating my first note. I pulled the microphone to my mouth and began to sing.

What happened then was nothing short of a miracle. All the fear just disappeared, and a sensation overcame me, unlike any other I had ever experienced. The microphone seemed to become an integral part of my hand, and my movements became fluid, one with the melody. The sound coming through the monitor was my voice, but it seemed different, unlike I had ever heard my voice sound before. There was no resonance of fear, and I heard beautiful, clear notes as they were expelled by my diaphragm to fill the auditorium. It was almost like an out-of-body experience. My song ended with a sustained note. The piano music ceased as my head bowed. It was dead quiet.

I raised my head as cheers and clapping exploded from the audience. I nodded in acknowledgement to the judges and quietly walked off the stage. Out of eyeshot of the audience,

February 22, 1975

I took a deep breath, as my knees began to uncontrollably shake. I could hardly balance myself as I looked for something to lean against. From behind me, a voice whispered, "Way to go, Beck." It was my friend, my accompanist. She smiled, gave me a hug, and then disappeared.

I had plenty of time to gain my composure as the pageant broke for an intermission. Backstage, in the dressing room, I engaged in friendly chatter with thirteen young women, as we prepared for the final phase of competition. We were all glad that the swimsuit and talent portions were behind us. It was crazy backstage as we all slipped on our evening wear and primped in front of the mirrors. There were hugs and words of encouragement coming from these young women, and I felt reassured that we *were* all winners. The door to the dressing room opened, and the stage coordinator announced that the music had begun. We were to take our places in the wings.

Evening gown competition was the easiest of all. I felt perfect in my special dress and my clear Lucite heels. The chiffon skirt floated like a cloud when I walked, and the color dazzled under the lights. I felt extraordinary when I stepped to the microphone and began to speak. Again, although I was scared, my voice gave the impression that I was confident. I was well aware that all eyes were on me as I did the appropriate turns and once again nodded to the judges.

After the evening gown competition, we were all summoned to return to the stage to stand, as the reigning queen said her good-byes and gave her congenial thank-you for her year's experiences. Again, my knees began to shake, and my lips started to quiver. Even though I knew that the competitions were over, I was scared. Scared to lose and scared to win. We waited and waited for the judges' final decision to come and for the announcement, "The envelope, please." Once again, my eyes fixed on the little girl in the back of the auditorium. I almost felt as though she and I had a sort of kinship. She will never know how much she helped me that night. Nor will I ever be able to thank her for just being there as my bright focal spot in that auditorium.

The emcee asked, "Judges, do we have a final decision?" There was a hand motion from the head judge, and the emcee crossed the stage in front of us and bent over as the envelope was handed to her. She crossed back to the podium at stage right and stood quietly as she opened the envelope. The announcement of the second runner-up was first, and then came the announcement of the first runner-up. The auditorium inflated with chatter and applause. Waiting for the crowd to quiet, the emcee turned to look at the remaining twelve girls. She smiled and turned back to the audience. "And the winner of a two-hundred-and-seventy-five-dollar scholarship, and Miss Helena 1975, is contestant number ten—Becky Clark!"

I stood motionless, not believing what I was hearing. Immediately tears filled my eyes as a crown was plopped on my head, a robe was slipped over my shoulders, and a bouquet of roses lay cradled in my arms. The music "Look at Her" swelled and I walked slowly down the small lighted runway. The lights dimmed on the stage, and the house lights were turned on, illuminating the audience. Finally, I could see my mom and dad, my grandparents, Jim and Eve, my friends, my sisters, and my brother. They were all standing and cheering for me. I smiled at the judges, silently thanking them for devoting their time. I turned and walked back to center stage, where my newfound friends greeted me with hugs, kisses, and tears. It was just like you see on television, only this was real. Turning my head, I noticed a dark figure just off the stage. It was Neil. He, too, was smiling.

I remember crawling into bed that night and lying in the quiet, waiting for sleep to come. I was exhausted from the emotional event. I woke several times in the night, making sure the flowers and the crown were really still on my dresser, hoping that my night had not just been a dream. It was one of the best experiences of my life and one that I will never forget.

MISS HELENA 1975!

This year's Miss Helena, Rebecca "Becky" Clark, 17, is crowned by last year's Miss Helena, Jocelyn Sajor, during award ceremonies following competition Saturday night at the Helena Junior High auditorium. Runners-up include: Linda Kleffner, first runner-up; Linda Osorio, second runner-up; Nicki Verploegen, third runner-up; and Karen Mulcahy, fourth runner-up. Miss Mulcahy also received the Miss Congeniality award. Award for the best non-finalist in the talent category went to Sherry Sparkman. (Staff photo by Ralph Barzditis)
*The Sunday Independent Record, Helena, Mont., Sunday morning, February 23, 1975

Where Am I?

Over the next couple months, I would prepare for the Miss Montana Pageant, to be held in Billings, Montana. The pageant director and his wife were good people, who were anxious to mold me and shape me into their perception of a queen. I allowed them to dictate changes, believing that they were certainly much more knowledgeable in this entire process than I was. The preparations for the state pageant were almost as grueling as conditioning would have been for a physical endurance race.

I was grilled on questions regarding current events. Many mock interviews were staged, so that I would be prepared for even the most scrutinizing interview. Mental exercises were given to me to teach me to formulate my answers in a strong, mature presentation. I was instructed on how to sit, speak, and walk.

I exercised daily, sometimes twice a day. There was no room for extra weight. My body had to be trim and fit. I ate like a bird, except for those times when Mom insisted, I eat a good meal. Thank God I never got caught up in purging or anything like that. The truth is, however, that I did develop an eating disorder. I just didn't like to throw up, but I could go for days without food of any sort, starving my body of necessary nutrients. When I pushed myself to the outer limits, I would become so weak that I would get dizzy when I stood up. I used to feel faint quite often. I was usually able to drop five, ten, or sometimes fifteen pounds in one or two weeks. And I was generally able to hide this from my mom and dad.

I sang my song, on average, two to three times per day. My stage movements were choreographed, and the lyrics became ingrained in my brain. I was coached, poked, and prodded. No longer did I feel fluid in my movements, and my song was becoming uninteresting and unfeeling.

I was told how to style my hair, wear my makeup, what kind of shoes would make my legs look leaner, how to smile so my cheeks didn't look fat, and how to walk tall like a queen. Before I knew it, I was becoming a shadow of the girl I once knew.

I was nervous about the state competition, but I think that I was so scared about making a mistake that I made myself ill. Mom finally had to intervene. One afternoon, she knocked on my bedroom door. I was lying on the bed, exhausted from school and the pageant and life in general! I said, "Come in."

She opened the door and peeked in. With a smile on her face, she entered, walked to my bed, and sat on the edge. She said to me, "You know, you won Miss Helena because you were you. Don't forget that. I know you have been working hard and have been forced to make lots of changes. Just be careful, honey, and don't let them change who you are inside. Okay?" Enough said, she smiled and walked out the door.

She was right. Some of the changes were good. Changes can be positive, but they can also be confusing, especially when there had been so many. I needed to get back to the basics and find the real me underneath all of the "fluff and stuff"!

The first thing I needed to do was to decide whether or not I really wanted to become Miss Montana. There was no sense in putting myself through all of this exhausting training and conditioning if I really had no desire to do this. Secondly, once I determined that I did, in fact, want to win, I had to tell the pageant committee that I needed to get back to being me. Thirdly, I needed to have the support of Neil in this endeavor. Once I knew that I was going for it, I needed him to endorse this thing and quit fighting me on it. I needed him to stop acting as if he were being ignored and neglected. I had to have his tolerance and acceptance, or it just wasn't going to work.

The pageant committee took me to several pageants in neighboring towns. They wanted to expose me to as many of the other contenders as they possibly could. Being only seventeen, I had not been many places in my life. Just traveling to these Montana towns, representing Helena, was a responsibility that I took very seriously. I was delighted to meet new people and was ever calculating, in my mind, the extent of my competition. In my preparation for the state pageant, I met all of the girls that I would be competing against. Well, all but one!

Supposedly, all of the local pageants were complete, and final preparations were being made for the state pageant. However, one afternoon my director informed me that there was a late local pageant being held that weekend in Missoula, Montana, and he wanted me to go. It was going to be a mini pageant. I questioned why they were allowing a local pageant to take place only two weeks before the state pageant. My director was not pleased but was careful not to say too much.

We arrived in Missoula early in the morning. There were only three girls competing. One of the contestants had been the first runner-up at the Miss Montana Pageant in 1974, just one year prior. That girl, Diana Pacini, was remarkable! She was an accomplished pianist. A college girl, she was graceful and poised, classic and intelligent, familiar with pageant ups and downs—*she* was competition! I remember my heart sank when they announced Diana as the winner. She was definitely going to season the contest.

I arrived in Billings one week before the pageant. We were herded around like prize livestock on display. Our schedules were filled with appearances, style shows, and interviews. We were always on the move. Salads and ice tea seemed to comprise the staple meal for beauty queens, and I found myself craving pizza, or chocolate, or anything that wasn't green! Believe it or not, even though the agenda was exhausting and unpleasant at times, I enjoyed the entire process. I gained a great deal of respect for the program and the people who so generously volunteered their time and energies. Diana Pacini and I became friends through the week, and that only proved to be confusing.

On the day of the pageant, with the beginning of the Miss America overture, the excitement crept into every corner of my being. I knew that my family and Neil were in the audience, as well as several friends who had journeyed to Billings to support me. I was representing my hometown, and I was determined to have the time of my life. Although it was exciting, I thought that nothing could quite compare to my first experience, when I had been crowned Miss Helena.

The Miss Montana Pageant was a spectacular show. It was choreographed to perfection and was a complicated show with trained technical and production crews. I was in the big time now! Again, I was one of the youngest contestants. There were eleven of us in all, representing towns all across the state of Montana.

Diana Pacini was crowned Miss Montana that night, and I was awarded a respectful Second Runner Up. I was disappointed but not necessarily with the fact that Diana had won. She was deserving of the title and was certainly as sweet as she was beautiful and talented. My disappointment was three-fold. Number one, I realized I didn't like losing. I wasn't a *poor* loser; I just didn't like it! Number two, I felt I really hadn't done my best in the competition. Something had held me back, and I couldn't put my finger on it. I hadn't delivered my song as powerfully as I knew I was capable of doing. I didn't feel that my interview went as well as it could have, either. And, number three, Neil was actually relieved that I didn't win. I could see it in his eyes. I remember him saying that he was proud of me but that things could now get back to normal.

Well, things did get back to normal for Neil. He entered the University of Montana on a full-ride football scholarship. And things got back to normal for our relationship too. We had a tumultuous relationship, and I was getting tired of always trying to please him and stay out of his way.

My Best Friend

I have often heard it said that if at the time of one's death a person has but one *true* friend, he or she is lucky. Well, I would almost agree with that statement—all but the "lucky" part. I believe that having a true friend is a divine blessing. I have been rewarded with the love of dear friends, and I have been cherished by some of the most incredible individuals in life. My dearest friends are like precious gems that glitter and sparkle in my memories. I have also been blessed with that one true friend. He is a man by the name of Chris Jacobson, known to his friends as Jake. He is my confidant, and I love him so much.

We met one night at a club in Missoula, Montana. It was a Friday night. My roommates and I usually went out on the weekends, taking a break from our college studies. We were regulars at the club; I actually hung with some very "happening" girls. They worked hard in school but, gosh, they played hard on the weekends. Chris was out with some of his friends that same evening. The year was 1977, and disco was the happening phenomenon all across the nation. The Acapulco had it all: a cool DJ, great bartenders, a lighted

Plexiglas dance floor, the finest music, polyester leisure suits, platform shoes, and dancing—lots and lots of dancing.

I loved to dance, and unfortunately, Neil hated to dance, especially at the discos. Neil's idea of going out on the town was drinking and partying with other football players. I enjoyed that sometimes, but there were occasions when being with Neil and his friends just put me in too close a proximity to major doses of testosterone.

One night I was out on the town with my girlfriends, and Chris spied me from across the dance floor. He questioned one of the friends he was with, asking them who I was. That friend indicated that I was the girlfriend of one of the football players and that I was more than likely off limits. Yet, Chris's friend did ask me to dance. While we were on the dance floor, he whispered in my ear and nodded toward Chris, explaining that his friend would like to dance with me. I remember smiling and looking his way, not ever imagining that this young man would touch my life in such a significant way.

Chris was tall and slender. He had beautiful eyes and a warm, inviting smile. He extended his hand out to me and escorted me to the dance floor. He was an incredible dancer; he knew all the latest moves and knew all the current tunes. He commanded the dance floor, much as John Travolta did in the movie sensation *Saturday Night Fever*. It was like the parting of the Red Sea when he took the floor. He was complimentary too, telling me that he thought I was a great dancer and that he found me very attractive. I remember blushing with a multitude of emotions surging through my body. I was nervous in an exciting sort of way, yet I felt very comfortable around Chris. After we danced, he invited my girlfriends and me to join him and his friends at their table.

We agreed, and for the rest of the evening we were treated to drinks, conversation, and dancing.

We talked as much as the loudness of the music allowed, getting to know one another under the silvery twinkle of the spinning disco ball. In a brief amount of time, I learned several things about him. He was from Jackson Hole, Wyoming, the son of a cowboy outfitter. His parents were divorced, and he had several siblings, all boys. He had needed open-heart surgery as a young child. Consequently, he had never been able to do athletics much as a kid, but he loved being around athletes and sports. He was studying to be an athletic trainer at the University of Montana. He admitted that he knew who my boyfriend was and that he didn't want any confrontation with Neil. In the same breath, however, he asked if he could drive me home. I don't know why I agreed to let him take me home, but before I knew it, we were in his car. Strangely enough, there was no awkward silence as we drove to my apartment. We continued our conversation from earlier that evening. It was as if we had known each other our entire lives.

When we arrived at my apartment, I invited him in, expecting that my roommates would still be partying. We visited with my friends for a while, but when they said good night and headed for bed, Chris stood to say good night. Surprising myself, I asked him if he could stay a little longer. I was really enjoying his company. We talked until the wee hours of the morning.

The next day there was a Grizzly football game. As a university cheerleader, I arrived at the game early and took my place on the sidelines. Across the field, I saw Chris as he accompanied the football team onto the sidelines, part of the training in his curriculum. He smiled at me, and I felt certain that he could tell from where he stood that my heart was racing. I was worried that Neil would see me interacting with this guy. But remember, Neil's focus was always on the game. He could have cared less that I was at the game, much less that I was on the sidelines flirting with some guy on the other side of the field.

I have no idea why Chris stayed my friend during this time in my life, other than it being a divine blessing. I needed his friendship, and I used that friendship to my advantage. Whenever I was feeling down or struggling in my relationship with Neil, I sought out Chris for comfort. He was my savior. He knew every painful story surrounding my relationship with Neil. He used to shake his head and tell me that things were never going to change until I had the courage to initiate the change. He treated me like a queen, and I dumped garbage on him continually. He never said no to my requests to come over. He always met me at the door with a smile and an outstretched hand. He sat and listened to me whine and wail, tenderly comforting me and holding me until I fell asleep. I loved him, but I never realized how very much I loved him until it was too late.

One evening, after a night of dancing, Chris and I went for a drive before he took me home. We went to a park area, stopped the car, and got out to go for a walk. We held hands as we walked along. Our pace slowed noticeably, and Chris breathed deeply before he began to speak. "I haven't been the same since we met. I am in this relationship for entirely different reasons than you are. I have this ridiculous hope that someday you will see something in our relationship that even slightly resembles an 'us.' But I realize now that I can't wait for that. Nothing is going to change. You're going to keep coming to me after fights with Neil and ask me what to do and tell me he's hurt you once again. What do you want from me? What am I supposed to think?" Stunned, I waited for the right words to come from my mouth. But they were nowhere to be found.

He was being so honest. I was being so unfair. But the truth was that I needed Chris in my life. He was kind and gentle and loving and always had time for me, no matter what day of the week it was or what time of the night. He never looked away from me or shunned me. I always felt better after being with him than I had before. I felt so loved when I was next to him.

Waiting for me to respond, he continued. "I can't do this anymore. I want you to be more than a friend to me. But I am convinced that you are willing to settle for the familiar. You know Neil. You know his family. Your family knows his family. You have a connection with him. You could never step out of those boundaries for me. I would be too much of a risk for you."

Dumbfounded, I tried to think of what I could say to make this right. "Chris, it's not that simple. You need to understand that I really do care about you, and I don't want to lose you. I want you in my life. I am sorry that I have been so selfish, but I never knew how you felt until now."

Well, that wasn't entirely the truth. I would have had to be blind not to see how he cared for me. But truth is, he was absolutely right. Neil was the familiar. Chris was definitely out of my comfort boundaries. How could I ever make the break in my relationship with Neil? Neil and I were not good for each other. It was plain to see. Yet, something tied me to him.

Thanks for the Memories

In October 1977, with encouragement from family and friends, I entered the Northwest Regional Talent Search at the University of Montana. The search was conducted to find new talent for the entertainment industry; it was an opportunity to appear on a proposed Bob Hope TV special, to air in the spring. All over the United States there were similar competitions being held. Winners from each college or university contest would then be entered into the next phase of competition. The United States had been divided into regions for the talent search. After each winner was selected, he or she would go on to join the regional winners in the national competition and would compete in Kansas City, Missouri. The national competition was going to be judged by Bob Hope himself. The top three winners of the national competition would be awarded recording contracts, advanced training, and the opportunity to be personally introduced to entertainers, agents, producers, and the like. They would also have the opportunity to join Mr.

Hope on the special. This competition could alter a person's life in a most powerful way.

I had talent. I didn't doubt that. I remember lying in my bed one night, and when I closed my eyes, I saw myself the winner. I could do this thing. I really could do this. I had encouragement from my folks, my roommates, Chris, other friends, and Neil. I even had the blessings of some of my professors in the music department.

The director of the Miss Montana Pageant sent me prerecorded music tapes for accompaniment. I chose to do a song from the Broadway Show *A Chorus Line.* "What I Did for Love" was a beautiful song about the life and emotions of a washed-up dancer with a tenuous future. I sang the song well, and I believed that it was a strong number for the contest.

When the day of the competition arrived, I was a nervous wreck. The contest was held at the commons on the campus. The room was packed and the stage was set. They would only be taking the top winner to the national contest, and I wanted to be that winner. Actually, I needed a lucky break. I just wanted to finally achieve one of my goals, that of becoming a vocal entertainer. That wasn't so much to ask, was it?

I was pleased with my performance; I even received a standing ovation. But I was also amazed at the quality of the other performers. I wouldn't have found it an easy task to judge. With the competition over, the announcement of the winner came. I came in second. A barbershop quartet had been chosen as a regional winner to represent the University of Montana. I had to admit that they were good. No, not just good—they were great. They deserved to win. Again, however, I felt like a failure.

Gary Bogue, from the ASUM Programming Office, approached me after the competition and said that he wanted to visit with me and two other contestants. We met in the programming office, and Gary explained how very close the competition had been. In fact, one other vocalist and I had tied for second place a mere five points behind the quartet, and the other vocalist had come in third place, only one point behind second. With 150 possible points, it had been very close. In conjunction with the search, the programming office was sponsoring "The Bob Hope Show" on December 2 at the Harry Adams Field House. Gary offered the other two contestants coffeehouse dates at the university commons lounge, and he also gave one of them the chance to be the opening act for John Lee Hooker, a prominent blues musician. The Hooker concert was in two weeks, and they would perform for a half hour and would be paid for their performance. Gary looked at me and said, "I've gotta think of somethin' for you. I'll be calling you tomorrow or the next day. If you don't hear from me, you call me. Okay?"

I smiled as a "sure thing" expression passed my lips. I thought to myself that he was just trying to appease me and that he really didn't have anything in mind for me.

Two days later, the phone rang. It was for me. "Becky, this is Gary Bogue with ASUM Programming. I have an offer for you, and I think you will be pleased. I just got off the phone with Mr. Hope's show producer. He asked me if I knew a talented young woman who would be willing to star with Mr. Hope here in December. I told him about you, and there is about a fifty-fifty chance that we can pull this all together. What do you think?"

I screamed, "Yes, yes! I would love to perform with Mr. Hope! When will I know?"

"Well, I'll keep you posted. I should be getting the music from Mr. Hope's producer for the Jazz Workshop to practice on within the next couple of days. I'll give you a call."

Well, needless to say, I hung up the phone screaming and jumping up and down! My roommates thought I was nuts. I dialed my parents' number and was so excited I could barely talk. I finally calmed down enough that I could tell them about the phone conversation I had just had. There was a chance that I was going to perform with Bob Hope! *Wow!*

As luck would have it, only two weeks before the show, Bob Hope's producer called Gary and said that Mr. Hope was bringing his own performer with him, and they wouldn't need me. She had performed with Mr. Hope many times before, and Mr. Hope felt more comfortable with this arrangement. Gary hated to have to tell me. Before he'd called me, he'd had a talk with Lance Boyd, the director of the Jazz Workshop.

Lance had said, "Boy, that's going to be a big blow to Becky. She has been working really hard on this music, for weeks. Hey, how about The Workshop accompanying her on a number to open the show, instead of just The Workshop doing the opening number? It would be great to showcase her talent, and I just know, having worked with her over the last month, that we could put something together quickly that would be a show-stopper."

Gary said, "Well, let's give it a shot."

I was disappointed with the phone call. Who wouldn't have been? But when Gary proposed doing an opening number for the show with The Jazz Workshop, I was flat-out excited and extremely flattered. "Two weeks!" I screamed. "We only have two weeks to put this together! What am I going to do?"

Gary answered, "Call Lance. You two need to work this out."

At that point, I thought that all those weeks of practicing those numbers had been a waste of time. What I didn't realize was that those weeks had given Lance a comfort level with me, and he knew for sure that the jazz musicians and I could do this thing.

Up until the very day of the Bob Hope show, Gary wasn't sure he was going to let the number stay in, because he hadn't seen it. At the afternoon dress rehearsal, he was very impressed with The Jazz Workshop. They had worked very hard on the music that Mr. Hope's producer had sent them.

Bob Hope, however, was not as impressed. He was a tyrant, throwing out rude and cynical comments. His producer said he was tired and jet-lagged. I just thought he was a nasty old man with a potbelly. I felt sorry for Lance and the musicians. They were doing a superb job, and he was so short of temper and so uncomplimentary. Well, luckily, Mr. Hope's portion of the rehearsal ended quickly. The celebs were escorted out of the field house and back to the hotel for their beauty rest. The barbershop quartet and a couple of other regional winners from other states rehearsed their numbers, working out the kinks with the soundman and the lighting technician.

Lance looked up the bleachers at me and motioned for Gary to come over. Lance said, "How about the kids and Beck show you the number they have been working on for the opening act? It'll knock your socks off!"

Gary nodded. "Let's hear it!" he said.

I had been keeping a pretty low profile during all of the rehearsing. Technically, I wasn't supposed to be in the field house until it was time for my number. Bob Hope's bodyguards had been very specific about that. Lance yelled from the music pit, "Becky, let's do this thing!"

I leaped up and ran down the steps of the bleachers, jumped up onto the stage, and said, "Ready when you are!"

The number was "Queen Bee," from the current remake of the motion picture *A Star Is Born,* starring Barbra Streisand and Kris Kristofferson. I had choreographed my number and had worked so hard to put the number together with The Jazz Workshop. That day we were in perfect time, and the number was done as close to perfection as possible. The number was not yet over when we were rudely interrupted by one of the members of the barbershop quartet. He had been watching from the bleachers, and he was hot!

In anger, he threw accusations at me, at Gary, at Lance, and at the musicians. "You lost the competition! Where do you get off thinking that you are going to perform in this show! You've got a lot of nerve!" I was aghast! Before I could get out of the way, a can of Coke struck the stage directly in front of me, exploding and spraying all over me and several of the musicians in the pit. I didn't see who had thrown it, but Gary grabbed the quartet member and escorted him past the other three members and outside. Hoping he would cool off, Gary came back inside and motioned for us to pick up the number where we had left off.

Shaken, I tried to focus on the number, but my concentration was broken when the angry kid reentered the scene. This time, Gary motioned for security, and I watched as he was ushered out of the facility and told not to come back. I stood there, not believing what had just happened. Why was he being so cruel? What had I ever done to him?

Gary stood quietly as he said, "Lance, I'd like to hear it from the top. Becky, when you gain your composure, I want to hear it again, okay?"

"Sure" was all I could say. I smiled at Lance and said, "The third time's a charm. I'm ready." The number came off without a hitch this time, and with the number complete, I searched Gary's face for some sort of a sign. Was he going to keep the number? Or was the earlier display of anger from the quartet going to determine his answer?

"Well," Gary began, "all I can say is this: You had better be that good tonight, or my ass is in a wringer!" And with a smile and a shake of Lance's hand, Gary began to walk away. Turning around, he yelled, "Be here by six o'clock tonight, and don't be late."

That evening, the field house was brimming with anticipation. The loud chatter diminished to whispers as the lights dimmed, and I took my place on the dark stage. The drumbeat began, and as I moved my hips to the rhythm, the lights hit the stage and bounced off my shiny black leather, sequined costume. My voice filled the vast arena with melodic sound, contrasting the heavy rhythmic reverberation of the drums and bass guitar. The music rose as the other instruments joined together in this perfect blend of instrument and voice.

For two minutes and forty seconds, I had the thrill of performing in front of my parents, Chris, my friends, my family, Neil—and six thousand other people. It was a rush! I remember every movement and every word, how the lights dazzled, and how the musicians made me sound. They were wonderful. Lance Boyd and the University of Montana Jazz Workshop were incredible. We were great together! I never thought the applause would stop, and as I walked down the steps in the darkness, reveling in the moment, I brushed my arm against Mr. Hope. He turned to me and said, "Pretty good for a kid."

From the sound system a voice clamored, "Ladies and gentlemen, please give a warm Montana welcome to Mr. Bob Hope!" I stood in the wings and watched as he climbed the steps to the music "Thanks for the Memory," and as the crowd roared, the lights illuminated the celebrity at center stage. And there he was, Mr. Bob Hope, beloved entertainer, comedian, & singer.

Rebecca Clark

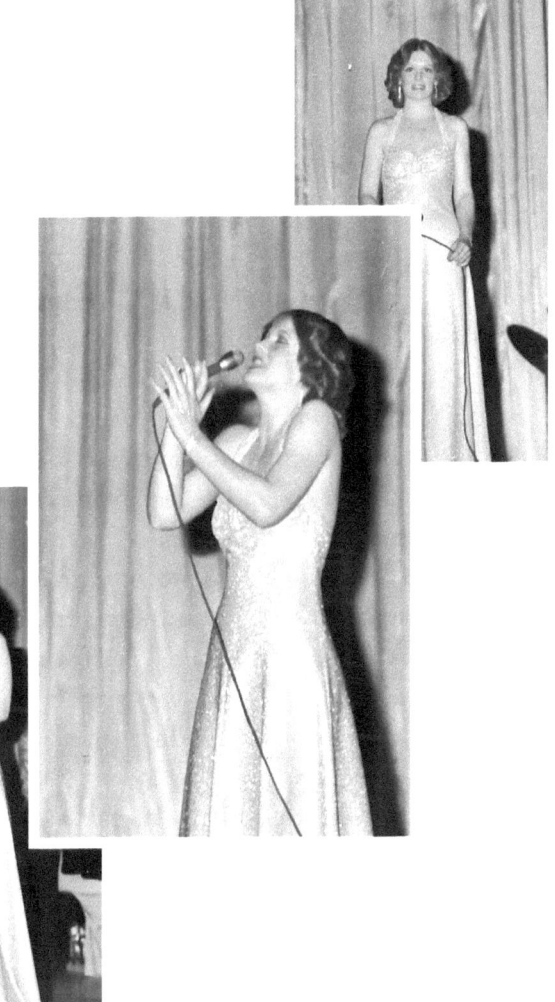

This Heart of Mine

I spent the summer of 1978 in Iowa and Nebraska with one of my college roommates, Lisa Altman. Her family owned a farm there, and I was eager to go anywhere to get away from Neil. We had been arguing and fighting, putting more strain on our relationship.

We were engaged to be married; however, our relationship had been on again, off again for months, and we had not been happy for quite some time. I was still living in Missoula, but Neil had transferred from the University of Montana to Carroll College, in Helena. I had decided to transfer to Montana State University in Bozeman for the following school year, and I didn't want to be anywhere near Neil for the summer.

I had a great time that summer, working hard and playing hard. But summer passed quickly, and Lisa and I returned to Montana. We drove straight through from Iowa to Montana. It was a long drive, and Lisa and I were exhausted by the time we reached our destination. I called my friend Chris to tell him I was home, and then I crawled into bed for a power nap.

I had to pack up my things and say good-bye to my roommates and head for Helena, where I would be staying with my folks for a few weeks before moving to Bozeman. It was hard to say good-bye to everyone, especially Chris. I knew that I would miss him. He was still my very best friend.

I don't know why I did it, but when I got to Helena late that afternoon, I drove directly to Neil's apartment. I hadn't spoken to him all summer, nor had I seen him in over three months. I don't know whether I missed him or if I just missed the routine of our relationship. Whatever the reason, I found myself walking up the steps to his apartment and knocking on the door.

One of his roommates answered the door, and I could hear laughing and loud music coming from inside. I said, "Hi. Um … I'm Neil's girlfriend, Becky. Is he here?"

"Yah, sure, let me get him." The door closed in my face, and I stood outside waiting.

When the door once again opened, there stood Neil. He looked great, and he smiled and said, "Hi! What a surprise. I wasn't expecting to see you." We managed to give each other a quick hug.

"Can we talk, Neil?" I questioned.

"Well, it's really not a good time just now. I have some friends over, and we are sort of having a party. Can you come back, maybe later this evening?"

Stunned by his cold reaction to seeing me for the first time in almost three months, I said, "Sure, maybe I can do that." I turned and walked down the steps as I heard the door close behind me.

I sat in my car for almost ten minutes, thinking to myself, "What the hell am I doing in this relationship? Why did I even come here? How can Neil be such a jerk?" I drove to my parents' house with tears streaming down my face.

My folks were so glad to see me. They both helped me unpack my car, and we sat around the dinner table, talking and laughing. They inquired about my summer and what I had done at the farm. I presented them with small gifts that I had purchased in the Midwest. It felt good to be home, safe and secure.

Pulling me aside, Dad asked me why I had been crying when I drove up. I explained to him that I had stopped to see Neil and that our short meeting had not been what I had expected. Dad hugged me and told me he loved me. Mom was furious that I had agreed to go back to town to see Neil later that evening. She didn't understand our relationship at all. She loved Neil, but she was concerned about us, about me. Join the club! I didn't know what to think of our relationship either. How could two people who supposedly loved each other so much be so distant? The truth was that being apart was the only reason we were still together. Does that make any sense?

Despite the objections of both my mom and dad, I got into my car and drove to town to see Neil. He actually seemed happy to see me this time. We talked about our summer, and he suggested that we step out to get a bite to eat. After dinner, we drove over to see Mom and Jim. It was a joyous reunion! I had missed them so much.

We arrived back at Neil's apartment quite late. Again, loud music and chatter came from inside the apartment. There were several people there that I had never met before; that was not surprising, as Neil and I had been apart for some time. We had several drinks and talked late into the night.

I was exhausted by the drive from Iowa and this, combined with the alcohol, made me feel uncomfortable to drive.

Neil convinced me to stay the night. I didn't feel safe driving home, so I called my parents. Mom sounded disappointed with me but thanked me for calling. She said, "See you in the morning?"

My Guardian Angel Is on Vacation

Mom and Eve accompanied me to Bozeman to find an apartment. We came upon a great little place that was affordable and clean, located in the basement of an older couple's home. They were rather strict in their rules and regulations, and I think my mother felt secure, knowing that I would be safe there.

Mom and Dad moved me in, wished me luck, and with a kiss, they were gone! I had never lived alone before. It was awful! The owners were nosy and very judgmental. I felt as though they were watching me every minute that I was there. They wouldn't allow me to listen to music past a certain time of night, and they always questioned my comings and goings. If I slept past eight o'clock in the morning, they would knock at my door to see if I was going to school. If, by chance, my phone rang later than they thought it should, they would mention it the next day.

One evening, I was at the library, studying for an exam with a classmate of the male gender. It was getting late, and we still had more to study, but the library just felt too stuffy. He lived with four other guys and said his place wasn't conducive to study. Our options were a restaurant or my place. Well, I lived alone and—what the heck—we would be quiet, and I could fix us some tea. I had a great kitchen table, and we could spread our books out. So, we agreed to meet at my house at eleven o'clock. I told Jerry to come up the alley, and I would just leave the door to my apartment open so he wouldn't have to knock or anything. That way he wouldn't disturb "big brother" upstairs.

Not long after he arrived, we were just beginning to study when there was a knock at my door. I peeked around the door from the kitchen, and there stood my landlady. I went to the door, where she proceeded to lecture me on having a young man in my apartment. I was so embarrassed and humiliated. I had a few words with her and shut the door in her face. She was still spouting off when I walked back into my kitchen. Jerry left my apartment around four o'clock in the morning. Our exam was at eight o'clock.

I showered and left for school. Not arriving home until quite late, I was surprised to find a note on my door. It was from my landlady. The note said that they had no intention of renting their apartment to a harlot. If I could not abide by their rule of not having male visitors, I would have to move out. I crumpled the note and slammed my door. It was Friday, and I had no intention to face them and have another confrontation, so I threw some things together, fed my fish, jumped in my car, and headed for Helena.

I didn't talk to my mom and dad about the incident. They didn't need to worry about that. I figured that it would all blow over, anyway. It was nice to be home, and I had quiet time to think and do some studying too. I hadn't heard from

Neil in almost three weeks, and I was not about to call him. So, I went to see Eve and Jim, but I stayed away from Neil.

Wednesday of the following week, I woke up early in the morning to study before going to class. I didn't feel well at all. I was tired and felt sick to my stomach. The feeling didn't leave me all day. In class, I commented to a friend that I was feeling a bit under the weather. He mentioned that he had had the flu all weekend and that several other people he knew had been sick. He said it was just a twenty-four-hour bug and that I should be feeling better by the next day.

By Saturday, I was still feeling awful. I was so tired, and I couldn't keep anything in my stomach. Even my landlords were concerned about me. They suggested I see a doctor on Monday, and they brought me ginger ale, crackers, and chicken soup.

I managed to pull myself out of bed on Monday for class, after which I went to student health services. I sat in the waiting room for about forty-five minutes to see a doctor. I explained to the doctor that I had been feeling very ill for a number of days, that I hadn't had a fever of any sort, but I thought that I probably had the flu. I told him that I had heard that it was going around campus. I asked him if there was anything that he could give me to settle my stomach. After listening to me for a few minutes, he peered over his glasses at me and said, "I'd like to test you to see if you are pregnant." I stared at him in disbelief. "You *could* be pregnant, correct? I mean, you are sexually active, right?" he inquired.

I sat motionless, as tears filled my eyes. Directing me to the lab for the test, the doctor placed his hand on my shoulder and said, "When you get the results, come back, and we'll talk."

I waited another hour before the nurse asked me to follow her. She led me into the doctor's office, and I sat for a few more minutes. Looking around the room, wringing a tissue tightly in my hands, I prayed a silent prayer. Entering the room, the doctor quickly went around to his desk to sit. Holding a paper in his hand, he looked across the desk at me and said, "Well, young lady, you don't have the flu. You are pregnant, and I'm guessing just about four or five weeks. So, technically speaking, you are still in an early enough stage to consider abortion."

I shook my head, no, as I said, "That's not an option for me." By that time, I was crying. The doctor said he understood and told me that I could remain in his office for a few minutes until I calmed down.

"If you change your mind about the pregnancy, you can come and see me." He left the room and as the door closed, I felt alone—so alone!

Gathering up my jacket and my backpack, I took a deep breath and opened the door. The hallway was extremely bright, and I felt as though all eyes were on me as I made my way toward the door. When I stepped outside, my tears turned to ice as they met with the fall chill in the air. I sat down on a bench outside the building and slipped on my jacket. Staring up at the afternoon sky, I became entranced as I watched a few tiny golden leaves float gently from the trees. I don't remember how long I sat there, collecting myself. After that, I remember walking for hours in the late, crisp, autumn afternoon and evening before returning to my apartment.

I was sitting at my table, eating a piece of toast, when my landlady once again knocked at my door, wanting to know where I had been. She asked how I was feeling. She informed me that she and her husband had been concerned about me and had thought that I was home, since my car was here. They had knocked several times on the door, and when I didn't answer, they had let themselves in. Finding that I was not there, they had just looked around, checking things out. They wanted to let me know that they were pleased with how clean I was keeping the place, especially how organized the cupboards were!

The cupboards? *That was it!* That was the last straw! I told them I was tired and not feeling well and that I wanted to be left alone. I was furious that they had gone through my private things. I didn't have anything to hide, but I did want my privacy! I shut the door and walked into my apartment. Looking around me, I found no comfort there, even being surrounded by my personal things. I sat on the edge of my bed, crying and wondering what to do next.

At about nine o'clock at night, I packed a small bag, grabbed a soda from my refrigerator and some crackers from my cupboard, and headed out the door. I taped a note to my door for my landlords. It read, "Gone to Helena—be back sometime this week." I jumped into my car, turned on the radio, and headed down the highway toward home.

It was close to ten thirty when I pulled into my sister's drive. Deb, her husband, and little girl lived on a farm close to Radersburg, Montana. I loved my sister very much, and my little niece was a precious baby. It would be great to see them, and I would feel safe there. There were no lights on in the house when I knocked on her back door. During the drive, I had gone over and over in my head what I was going to say to her. A light appeared through the window, and I heard footsteps from inside the house.

At first Deb's face lit up when she saw me through the window. But her smile quickly turned to a frown as she opened the door and said, "What are you doing here at this hour, and on a Monday? What's wrong?" Immediately I started crying, and she hugged me.

Still uncertain what was wrong, Deb tried to comfort me with a cup of tea and loving words. Not wanting to wake the baby, we both sat in the pale light talking in whispers. She fixed me a bed on the sofa while I washed my face. She looked tired and concerned, but she wasn't pushing the issue about what was wrong. Staring at the teacup I held in my hand; I told her that I had just found out that I was pregnant. She reached her hand out to me and then pulled me close. She said that, no matter what happened, things were going to be all right. Tucking me in, she kissed my forehead and shuffled back to bed.

The sun peeked through the windows of the farmhouse and I woke to the smile of my little niece as she crawled up on the couch to greet me. The house was quiet and chilly as she snuggled in next to me. I squeezed her tightly, and she drifted off to sleep again.

I stayed with my sister until early afternoon, then kissed her good-bye, and once again headed for home. The drive to Helena took me past the road to the ranch. I had not been there for years, and I don't know why I felt compelled to see it right then, but I turned my car at the sign and drove down the dusty road toward the ranch.

The road was bumpier than I had remembered. The jostling, coupled with my nausea, was not a good thing. I pulled my car around the drive to the barnyard. The place appeared much the same as I remembered. The big house was in need of some fresh paint, but from across the yard, it still looked like home.

As I rounded the corner, the trees, much taller than I had remembered, blocked the view of the houses. At the end of the line of trees was the well. Uncontrollable tears welled in my eyes as I slowed the car to a stop. Before me was my apple tree. It had grown taller and wider and had twisted with age, but it was still the beautiful tree I had loved as a child, and looking at it now somehow made me feel better.

The ranch seemed quiet when I stepped from my vehicle. I breathed a deep breath of fresh Montana air and tipped my head back to look at the clear Montana sky. Closing my eyes, I stood there for a while, taking in the silence and the fresh air. Then, not wanting to disturb anyone or to trespass, I got back into my car and drove away.

The dust from the road created a haze, blocking the view in my rearview mirror. As the ranch faded from my sight, the task ahead of me loomed in the distance. I had to tell those I loved that I had made a choice, a decision, and the consequence was growing inside me. I needed a thousand angels sitting on my shoulder just then. I turned up the radio and sped my car toward home.

From this Moment

When I arrived in Helena, I immediately drove to Neil's apartment. He was home, but he wasn't alone. Standing outside his door, I once again heard music and loud voices. I wondered whether he partied all the time or I just had bad timing. This time he answered the door himself. He was surprised to see me on a weeknight, all the way from Bozeman. I told him we needed to talk. He must have sensed the urgency of my request; he invited me in.

There were several members of the college football team in his living room, so Neil motioned for me to follow him down the hallway. His apartment was pretty small, so the only place really private enough to talk was in his room. We sat on the bed together. "What's up?" he questioned.

Turning to look at him, I began slowly. "Neil, I am pregnant. I just found out about this yesterday. I needed to tell you."

He sat there quiet and still for a moment before looking at me. "What are you going to do?"

The *you* in that question was not what I wanted or needed to hear. "What do you mean, what am *I* going to do? This is about us! This is about you and me!" I stammered.

"Oh, I know. I didn't mean it how it must have sounded. I meant to say, what are *we* going to do?"

"I don't know, Neil. All I do know is that I'm having this baby, so *we* need to decide how we are going to handle this. *We* need to talk to our parents tonight. Will you come with me?"

Neil didn't know what to say. He was ghostly pale as he reached for me. He held me close to him, rocking me back and forth, while saying, "I'm sorry. I'm so sorry."

Leaving his apartment, we drove across town to his parents' house. His mom met us at the door. She had a concerned look on her face when she saw me, but she hugged me tightly. She and I had never had difficulty talking, and she always had a wonderful way of relieving tension. A spot of tea was a staple at their house, and I was grateful when the teakettle whistled from the kitchen.

Exhausted from a busy day, Jim was resting in their bedroom. Neil asked his mom if she would go and get him. She looked puzzled but left the room to get him. It was several minutes before she returned with Jim by her side. Seated next to me on the sofa, Neil began the conversation.

"Mom and Jim, you know the problems that Beck and I have been having? You know we haven't been getting along very well. Well, we have another problem."

Jim looked across the room at us as he spoke. "Is this a *growing* problem?" he inquired.

Neil shook his head yes.

Eve's eyes lit up, and she jumped up and down as she shouted, "I'm going to have a grandbaby! I'm going to be a grandma!" She ran to me, hugging and kissing me, and then to her son, hugging and kissing him.

After she had settled down some, Jim asked me if my parents knew. I said no, but that Neil and I were going up to the house to tell them once we left there. Jim and Eve said that they would help us any way they could. Once we made a decision on what we were going to do, they would be there for us.

I was relieved at the reaction from Jim and Eve, but as Neil and I drove up the mountainside to my folks' house, my stomach began to churn. My mom and dad were both standing in the front room, looking out the window, as we drove up. They lived in the mountains, way up on a hill, and could hear the motor of any car that turned up the drive. They were wondering who was paying them a visit so late on a weeknight. It was about eight o'clock. They both looked disturbed when they saw that it was my car.

Neil and I walked up the path to the house as they opened the door to greet us. Dad looked confused. Mom looked worried. I looked scared and pale. Neil was confused, worried, scared, and pale.

Once inside the house, we were again offered a cup of tea. I went to the kitchen with Mom, and Neil sat in the front room with Dad. I chatted with my mom for a few minutes while we waited for the water to boil, and I could hear my dad and Neil making small talk in the other room. Mom and I carried the tea into the living room, and before I could sit, Dad spoke.

"Well, I'm guessing you didn't drive all the way from Bozeman this evening just to have tea with your mom and me. Is there something we need to know? Is there something you kids need to talk to us about?"

Neil looked at me with those beautiful gray-blue eyes as he began to speak, very slowly. "Mom, Dad, Beck and I have something very important to tell you. We are going to have a baby." A silence gripped the four of us as we sat looking at one another.

Breaking the uncomfortable silence, Dad quietly said, "Well, seeing that you two have been together for so many years, I'm not surprised. It's too bad it had to happen this way, but you know we can work this out."

I looked over at Mom. She had a strange look on her face, one that I had never seen. She hadn't spoken a word. "Mom, aren't you going to say anything?" I asked.

Coldly, she muttered. "Well, those tests aren't always right; maybe it's a mistake."

"No, Mom," I assured her. "It's no mistake. The doctor thinks I am about four or five weeks along. I'm sorry, Mom. It's true."

She rose from her chair and walked out of the room, saying nothing, not even looking at me.

Daddy shook his head, no, at me as I stood to follow her. He said, "Leave her, Beck. She just needs some time. I'll talk to her." It wasn't the reaction I had hoped for from my mom, but I suppose I should have expected it. My mom didn't handle disappointment well when it concerned her children—especially when it involved me.

Dad kissed me good-bye and shook Neil's hand. I told Dad that I would spend the night with Jim and Eve and I would be home for dinner the next night. He waved good-bye from the front porch. I turned around before the car headed down the hill, and I saw Mom standing in the window with her arms folded.

No Turning Back

I returned to Bozeman the following week. Still suffering from nausea, I became fatigued, and I found myself grabbing sleep whenever and wherever I could. My studies suffered tremendously. I was under extreme pressure in my classes, and I was becoming depressed and despondent. I was skipping classes, sometimes staying in bed for entire days. I ignored the knocks at my door and turned off the ringer of my phone. I was hardly eating. My skin was pale, and I was getting weak. When the weekends came, I would pack a small bag and drive to Helena, wanting to escape the depression, not knowing I was driving right into the storm.

I shall never forget the weekend that I announced to my parents that I wanted to drop out of school and return to Helena. I told them I was not doing well in school and that I couldn't survive alone in Bozeman. My mom was used to me being an A student and could not believe what she was hearing. Her dream had been for me to graduate from the university, and she was disheartened by my decision.

Looking at me, however, it was obvious that I was not handling my life well at all. I had lost almost twenty pounds, between the nausea and vomiting and the loss of my appetite. I had lost my sparkle and zest, and I honestly didn't care whether I flunked out of school or not. I felt so alone in Bozeman.

Neil sometimes called me during the week, but most of the time I had to wait until I came home on the weekends to even talk to him. His life included his football career and his studies and really hadn't even skipped a beat. He still partied with his friends and simply fit me into his schedule whenever it was convenient. We continued to argue and fight, and I realized more and more every day that he really didn't want or need me in his life right then.

Between his busy calendar and our arguments, we started making plans for the wedding. I always thought planning my wedding would be exciting and fun. Instead, it was dreadful! Nothing felt right. I was so sick and felt like such a failure for having withdrawn from school—not to mention that I felt I was a disappointment to my mom.

Keeping my pregnancy in mind, we decided on the date of December 16, 1978 and agreed to have a late-afternoon wedding. It would be before the holidays and well before I would be showing. We secured the church and arranged for Jim to perform the ceremony for us. Seeing as it was a quickly planned event, I knew that we would be operating on a somewhat tight budget. Mom and Dad certainly wanted my wedding day to be special, but we would simply have to be frugal and make every penny count.

Jim was the dean and rector of St. Peters Cathedral. Our indiscretion had placed him and Eve in a very awkward position, but I never felt as though they were ashamed of us. Jim told us that we needed to begin our premarital counseling sessions as soon as possible with one of the associate priests, Father Dan Semsch.

Our first meeting with Father Dan was more or less an introductory meeting. He learned a little more about Neil and me, including the fact that I was pregnant. His concern was that we enter into marriage for the right reason and not simply because I was pregnant. He wanted to make sure that we were ready for the commitment of marriage in addition to having a baby on the way.

At our second visit we were given a compatibility test. We were given the same test in different rooms. Then we were brought together to discuss our answers. It was a survey to find out whether we had the same goals, ideas, and desires for our future together.

The discussion seemed to be going okay until Father Dan asked, "Becky, what are the three most important things in your life at this moment in time?"

I responded, "Well, first and foremost, my faith in God is of the utmost importance. I know my trust in Him is the only thing that has gotten me through some very tough times in my life, and I believe He will get me through this too. Secondly, I love Neil and want to spend the rest of my life with him. I know we have some challenges to face, but I do sincerely love him. Then, I would have to say that the third-most-important thing in my life is this child I am carrying. I want to be a good mother."

"Okay," he said. "Now, Neil, please answer that same question for me."

Neil sat quiet for a moment, and then he looked at Father Dan as he began to speak. "I would have to agree with Becky that the Lord is first in my life. At this moment in my life, the second-most-important thing would have to be football, and third is my education, because that's going to get me where I need to be in life so that I can provide for a family."

The cold silence in the room was smothering. I sat there feeling that I had just been kicked in the stomach. I waited for some direction from the priest's counsel; I waited for a word or a nod. There was nothing. I didn't know if I was supposed to respond, and if so, I didn't know *how* to respond. I didn't know what to say. I didn't know how to feel. I didn't know how to react!

"Where am I in your list of important things, Neil? Am I even in the top five? How can you sit in the same room and say what you just said?" Raising my voice, I repeated, "How can you say that?" Father Dan looked at us, glancing from one to the other. My face became flushed as my disbelief turned into anger. I stood and said, "I don't want to talk any more. I am very upset and I am leaving." I did just that. I left Neil sitting there in the priest's office.

I clutched the steering wheel as Neil's words rang through my head. *Oh God!* My hand on my stomach, I looked down as I asked, "Oh, little one, what are we going to do?"

I drove to Jim and Eve's. They weren't home from work yet, so I let myself in with my key. The house was quiet as I walked back to the guest bedroom where I had been staying for the past couple of weeks. I crawled into bed, pulled the covers up over my head, and cried. I wanted the world to just go away for a while.

I must have drifted off to sleep. I was awakened by Eve as she gently whispered in my ear, "Dinner is ready, Keet. You need to get up, honey, and eat something." I was first anointed "Bequita Banana" by Neil's little brother, Glen. It was soon abbreviated by Eve to "Keet".

I smiled a faint smile and told her that I would be right there. Staring at myself in the bathroom mirror, I was horrified to see the dark circles under my eyes. I was so pale and tired. I just wanted to go back to bed.

The smells of dinner floated down the hallway, and I found the aroma comforting. I even felt a little hungry. I saw that the table was already set and, out of the corner of my eye, I noticed Neil sitting in the living room, talking to Jim. I sat down at the dining table and waited for everyone else to sit. We all sat there very quietly before Neil's brothers began conversation by talking about their days at school. Their dialogue was a welcome break in the silence. I couldn't even look at Neil.

With dinner over and the boys excused from the dinner table, Jim brought up the afternoon's counseling session. He suggested that we talk about it. The conversation turned into a heated argument between Neil and me. It wasn't long before I was crying hysterically and headed for the door. Outside, the wind was blowing the snow that had covered the ground. I didn't have a coat or boots on, but I started running toward the vacant lot, headed for the railroad tracks. I could hear Eve as she called me, but I kept running. The wind stung my face, and the tears burned my eyes. My feet became wet and cold as I trudged through the drifted snow in the dark. It wasn't long before I heard a vehicle behind me. It was Eve. She had come after me. The car stopped, and I heard her voice as she begged me to get in the car. I turned and walked toward her. She put her arms around me and helped me into the car.

Back at the house, she ran a warm bath for me, brought me a cup of hot tea, and then tucked me into bed. She said that things always looked better after a good night's sleep, and she tried to reassure me that tomorrow would be brighter.

Something Old, Something New

I had always wanted to wear my mother's wedding dress. It had been purchased at Rogene's Dress Shop, an exclusive shop in Helena in the 1950s. I remember trying it on when I was in high school, vowing to resurrect it when I married. At that time, I don't think that my mother thought I was really serious about wearing it. I believe that she was pleased, however, that I still wanted to wear her dress now, and I felt honored.

Mom had been quite a bit slenderer through the waist than I was, but there was plenty of room in the seams to let the dress out a bit. Mom chose to wait to alter the dress until the wedding was closer. I guess she was anticipating my expanding waistline.

Fashioned of ivory slipper satin contrasted with white, it was an exquisite garment. Fitted at the waist, with soft fabric draping off the shoulders, it looked like a *Gone with the Wind* gown. The top of the dress, to the shoulders, was gauze-like netting with satin trim at the neck. Old fashioned, delicate lace embellished the draping fabric on the bodice. The back of the dress was adorned with tiny satin-covered buttons, and it had a small train that made me feel like royalty when I walked. Beautiful gauntlet sleeves with delicate lace accentuated the dress. It was all too perfect!

Neil and I decided on colors for the wedding. As it was close to the Christmas holiday, we wanted colors that fit the season. However, I wasn't fond of red, so I chose a rose pink instead, with dark holly green. My attendants would wear the pink, and the gentlemen would wear the green.

The flowers would be simple, as the altar at St. Peter's Episcopal Cathedral would be beautifully adorned with poinsettias for the season. We wouldn't need any other flowers for the church. My bridesmaids would carry a single flower, and the men would have simple boutonnieres. I contacted my aunt in Seattle and asked her if she would send fresh holly for decorating the reception hall and the cake. She was delighted to do so.

Longing to bring a touch of his Scottish heritage to our wedding, Neil requested that we have bagpipes. I thought this sounded very appropriate for the season, and I knew that his grandmother and his father would appreciate it. Jim and Eve contacted a piper whom they knew from church. We were delighted when we heard that this man had accepted the invitation to play at our wedding. He even agreed to play the processional. He was an incredible artist and would be a fascinating addition to our wedding. The regular church organist also agreed to play, so the music was taken care of.

Neil asked his one of his brothers to be his best man and his other brother to be an acolyte, assisting Jim in the ceremony. He asked his best friend from college to stand up with him too. I wanted my two precious nieces to be flower girls and my little nephew to be the ring bearer.

I guess I just assumed that my sisters would be in my wedding too. After all, I had been in their weddings. I told them that Mom and I had picked out the dress pattern and the fabric for the bridesmaids' dresses. I mentioned that I just couldn't choose which of them I wanted to be matron of honor, so I was just going to have both of them assume that role.

I was devastated when they both declined! Neither one of my sisters wanted to be in my wedding party. First, Pam said that she didn't want to because she was pregnant. Pregnant? Okay, so what? She was only about three weeks further along than I was. Deb then told me that if Pam wasn't going to be in the wedding, she wouldn't either. It was a real blow to me. All of my life I had planned for my sisters to be a special part of my day, and now neither one of them would be. They both agreed, however, that they would make the dresses for the flower girls.

So, I picked myself up, brushed myself off, and asked my best girlfriend, Maureen Oelkers, to be my matron of honor. She lived in Kentucky and would be eight months pregnant by the wedding. She asked me if I was sure I wanted her in my wedding while pregnant. I said, "Absolutely! Join the party!" Maureen said yes! I also asked my friend, Lisa. She also consented, so I had my two attendants. They both agreed to have their dresses made, so I sent them the patterns and the fabric.

With the invitations out and the plans coming along, all I had to do was wait out the miserable morning sickness. It *never* went away. Why did they call it morning sickness, anyway? I was sick from morning to night; some days were worse than others were. I finally did go to the doctor and got something for the vomiting. It helped settle my stomach some and I stopped losing weight and started growing.

The wedding was set for four o'clock. At one thirty, my parents and I frantically stared at our watches. Eve was supposed to have met us at my mom's office building two hours earlier to decorate. It was no surprise that she was late, but on this special day I had hoped that she might be on time. She had the holly, which my aunt had had shipped to her house.

Finally, at one forty-five, Mom looked at Dad and said, "We have to be going. We have to drive all the way back to the house, pick up the wedding dress, get dressed ourselves, and get to the church by three thirty. We'll never make it unless we go now." We were just getting in the truck when Eve drove up.

She apologized for being late, and I know that I shouldn't have been angry, but I was. It was my wedding day, and I was going to be late! Hurriedly we threw the decorations together at the reception hall, jumped in the truck, and sped toward the mountains to the house. We just left Eve at the building with the key to lock up.

By the time we arrived back at the church, people were already seated and the music had started. I wasn't even dressed. Everyone else was there. It was about ten minutes before the wedding was to start. I was a nervous wreck! Maureen and Lisa were there. Deb, Pam, and the little kids were all there too. I was shaking like a leaf, when Mom told me to calm down. She said that it wouldn't be the first time a wedding was started late.

We quickly got me dressed. My hair, styled earlier in the day, looked a fright. Great! I was late for my own wedding and I was having a bad hair day to boot! Mom helped me freshen up my hair and she placed some baby's breath among the curls, as I sipped on some soothing tea. It wasn't long before I was calmed down and ready to go. It was ten minutes after four o'clock.

There was a knock at the door. It was Father Dan wanting to know when we would be starting the procession. He said that folks were getting restless. He continued by saying that he realized Neil was late, but did I know where he was? *Oh, no!* This was news to me and not good news either! I had thought that he was already at the church. Now I started to get anxious and worried all over again. Another knock came at the door. Good news—he was here!

My desire was to have both my parents accompany me down the aisle. I wanted my dad to give me away, but I wanted my mom to walk with me too. I remember standing at the back of the church, holding on to my parents, and saying to myself, "Well, this is it. This is the "something new" for my life. A wife and a mother—how much newer could something get?"

By that time, it was four thirty. The church was packed as we walked toward the front. Everyone was standing as I passed. I don't remember seeing anyone's face. Everything seemed just a blur. I do, however, remember the sound of the bagpipes and how extremely warm the church was.

I had made a secret arrangement with the organist, Imogene, to surprise Neil by singing a song to him, but I didn't know whether I could actually pull it off or not. I wasn't sure if my emotions would be in check during the ceremony. She would be watching for my signal. I would let her know whether I was going through with it or not. Standing before God and a church full of people, I gave Imogene the go-ahead. The music began, and I turned to face Neil. I had not looked at him face to face yet that day. I was shocked when I turned and stared into the bloodshot eyes of my hungover future husband. He looked awful. It was painful to even look at him while I sang. It made my eyes water. Evidently, he and his buddies had celebrated his last night of freedom, and he had definitely overindulged.

I don't remember much of the ceremony after my song. I recall exchanging our vows and the gentle touch of Jim's hand on my head as he blessed me, but everything else was a blur.

We had a receiving line at the church, where we served the wedding cake, punch, and coffee. The party with the food and alcohol was held later in the basement of my mom's office. We had the small reception at the church so we could visit with the older folks, family, and friends. The traditional receiving line was nice and gave us the opportunity to welcome everyone and thank them for coming. Then, of course, we had to go back upstairs for the pictures. We engaged in the cutting of the cake and the time-honored stuffing of a piece in each other's mouth.

After a couple of hours, the hall began to empty of guests, and we prepared to leave for the party. I remember walking up to Neil to tell him that I was going to change into my going-away dress. He had a stupid look on his face, and he said, "Well, do you think you can get a ride with someone? I'm riding with my buddy, so I'll see ya there!" Yes, this actually came from the mouth of my newly married husband! I fought back the tears as he left.

Yes, he left me at the church to find my own ride to our reception. I went to the pre-ceremony room and changed my clothes, grabbed my things, and walked out to find only a few of the church ladies left in the hall, cleaning things up. But I spied my mom and dad seated in the corner, waiting for me. They were smiling, in spite of the fact that they were angry and shocked that Neil had left me there.

Daddy took my bag from me and put his arm around me, saying, "Goin' our way?" I hugged them both and crawled into the pickup. We were quiet as we drove to the reception.

Photo of my wedding to Neil S Campbell
December 16, 1978

Something Borrowed, Something Blue

We arrived at the reception to find the party well under way. My aunt and uncle had arrived early to open up the room, and the food had already been laid out.

I don't remember any of my party reception, either. I did get to give my grandparents hugs and kisses out in the hall as we arrived. I said hello to some people taking off their coats, and then I followed my mom and dad into the room. I felt invisible. No one seemed to even notice me. Neil and all of his friends were at the corner bar, laughing and visiting. Many of our guests and relatives were standing in line for food or visiting among themselves.

I was standing next to a table and talking to some people, and the next thing I knew I was being abducted. Yes, a bride's worst nightmare. I was kidnapped from my own wedding reception. Literally, I was thrown over someone's shoulder and carried out of the building, kicking and screaming. Nobody came to my rescue, not even Neil.

Several of Neil's friends had conjured up the plan to steal me from the reception. I was not happy, nor was I pleasant. They took me to a bar downtown and sat me in the middle of a booth. Every attempt I made to get away met with resistance. If I got up to go to the ladies' room, they accompanied me. I was angry as I watched the time slip away. Finally, after two hours, they gave in to my tears and requests to take me back.

I came back to the reception only to find that all of our guests had gone. I had missed the entire party. I was starving, and I was crying. I didn't even get to say good-bye to some of the folks who had traveled so far to come to my wedding. I didn't get to visit with my grandparents or Neil's grandma or my friends.

Mom and Dad had been concerned about where I had been, but Neil hadn't even missed me. Mom fixed me a plate of food, and I sat down to eat as I watched while my family and Neil's family cleaned and put things away. I helped clean up and carry our wedding gifts to my sister's car.

I was exhausted and surprised when Neil told me of the plan for our evening together. He and his friends were going out. At least I was included in the plan, but I wasn't too excited about it. I do admit I had a good time dancing and laughing with our friends, but I watched with trepidation as Neil continued to drink. Consequently, we closed down the bar.

It was almost two o'clock in the morning when we finally got to our motel room. Neil, quite inebriated, simply crashed on the bed. Mom had given me a beautiful nightgown for my wedding night, so I grabbed my bag and told Neil I was going to go into the bathroom to freshen up. As I brushed my hair, I reflected on the day, and I can honestly say that I was glad it was over. I was too tired to be angry. I just wanted to crawl into bed next to my new husband. I opened the bathroom door and walked around the corner, only to find a snoring, drunken, passed-out husband. I sat on the edge of the bed, dressed in my sexy nightgown. I tried to wake him, but he didn't stir.

Needless to say, my wedding night wasn't glorious. I spent the night listening to Neil snore while I watched John Wayne's movie *Big Jake*. After sitting up all night, I showered and dressed and waited for the sun to stream in the windows.

The Mouse

Neil had college final exams the week after we were married, so we didn't go anywhere for a honeymoon. He promised me that we would take a trip somewhere after school was over. We had bought a nice mobile home from my parents, the one that they had lived in while they were building their new home. It sat in the court that Grandpa and Grandma Smith owned. Like most newlyweds, we didn't have much, so it was nice that the home was furnished. Neil and I worked at making our new surroundings comfortable.

I got a job working for the State of Montana in the Workers' Compensation division. It was an entry-level position, but it was a job nonetheless, and it helped pay the bills and put food on the table. Neil attended college and worked on the weekends at a dairy, delivering to grocery stores. During the week, after school, he spent a great deal of time with his friends. We only had one vehicle, so he would drop me off at work with the promise that he would pick me up at five o'clock. Many times, he wouldn't be there, and I would be left standing outside my office, waiting. On many occasions I called my mom and dad to come and get me.

As the weeks and months went by and my pregnancy progressed, I became less and less tolerant of his excuses. It was very obvious to me that I was still somewhere on the bottom of his priority list. An afternoon of snow-skiing or drinking with his friends always came first. Our relationship continued to crumble. I was fortunate to have my parents and my grandparents living so close. I didn't complain to them, but they knew that things were not going well.

I didn't really enjoy the whole pregnancy thing, either. I was still experiencing morning sickness through my eighth month, and I knew the true meaning of the term *heartburn*. I felt fat and sluggish and unattractive. My breasts hurt, my legs and feet hurt, my back hurt, and I was tired all of the time. Working was difficult, but I knew that I had to work. We had to have my income in order to survive.

One evening, after a quarrel, Neil left the house for a while to cool off. I waited up for him, hoping that we could apologize to each other. It was storming out when he finally got home. I had been worried about him as I'd listened to the wind howl and watched the snow swirl along the ground from the kitchen window. I met him at the door, and we hugged each other. Tired, we crawled onto the bed, and it wasn't long before Neil was fast asleep and began to snore.

The storm finally subsided and the moon peeked from behind the clouds. I hadn't slept and was uncomfortable, so I rose to change into my nightclothes. As I opened the closet and reached for a hanger, I saw something move. As quick as lighting, something ran over my hand. Not thinking clearly, I thought to myself, "Was that a snake? No, it was a lizard or something like that." Right! In the middle of a Montana winter, it was highly unlikely that the culprit was a snake or a lizard. I turned on the light and revealed the intruder.

There he was, sitting on the top of the closet rod, staring at me with his beady little eyes. The small mouse wiggled his rodent nose and scurried down some clothes. I screamed. He startled me; I startled him. He went one way and I went the other. Neil had no idea what was happening, except that his very pregnant wife was jumping around and screaming. I finally managed to scream the word *mouse!* By that time, I was standing on the waterbed. I watched as the small creature scampered through the open bedroom door and headed out to the living room. I pointed and shouted, "There he goes, Neil. Get him!"

Neil, standing in his boxer shorts, grabbed a ski pole from the closet and the Sears catalog from the nightstand. Armed with this ridiculous arsenal, he sprang into action.

"Where is he, Beck?"

"I don't know, but I'm not getting down until you find him!"

From the living room, I heard grunts and loud noises, then silence. I stepped down from the bed and carefully walked through the door to the living room. There, in a dark corner, Neil was postured like a great white hunter. He looked ridiculous, and I could not help but laugh.

Soon we were both laughing as the mouse headed for the kitchen. Frantically searching for a hiding spot, he barely escaped the *splat* of the catalog on the floor. Under the stove he went as the ski pole was launched like a spear from a mighty warrior.

Neil waited, staring at the stove. I got tired of watching for the mouse to reappear, so I went to bed. In the morning, I found Neil sleeping on the sofa next to his weapons of battle. I quietly slipped by him as I headed for work through the back door.

Little Miss Magic

The birth of my daughter, Megan, was a magical time for me. The discomfort of eight months of morning sickness, of feeling fat and unattractive, of my back hurting, and the pain of labor and delivery became only distant memories when I held her in my arms for the very first time. She looked so fragile when the nurse placed her on my stomach. I had loved her from the moment I knew she was growing inside of me, but to see her and touch her was an unbelievable moment in my life. Her tiny little body was red and wrinkled, and her little feet were long and bluish in color. She was crying at the top of her lungs but was quieted with my touch. She was so tiny, and I remember thinking to myself as the nurse handled her, "Be careful! That's my baby!"

Megan Rebecca Campbell, my truly special gift, was born June 13, 1979, at 6:13 in the morning and weighed six pounds and thirteen ounces. Consequently, the numbers six and thirteen became rather significant to me from that day forward!

Neil was enamored with his beautiful baby girl. The big, burly football player totally melted when he held her in his arms. For the first day or so of Megan's life, however, he chose to celebrate the event by drinking. He and his best friend came to see me the evening Megan was born, and I didn't see him again until a day and a half later.

When home, Neil was quite attentive to his new little one. There was no doubt that he loved Megan, but at this time in his life, the last thing he wanted was a family. I spent much of my time home alone or with Mom and Dad, Jim and Eve, or my grandparents.

After five short weeks of maternity leave, I returned to work. It was difficult to leave Megan, but Grandma and Grandpa Smith wanted to care for her. Every morning, I would walk across the yard with my sleeping baby and place her in the arms of my grandma.

Grandma and Grandpa loved her so much and were incredible with her. Grandma had given Megan her very first bath. Megan laughed for the first time at their house; she took her first steps at their house and spoke her first words there too. And although it was really painful for me to miss all those firsts, at least they were shared with her great-grandparents.

Grandpa Stan spoiled Megan rotten, allowing her to do things that he would never have let any other child do. She even got to sit in his special chair. Because of her tiny little lungs, he was even more restrained in his smoking habits. Megan brought a sparkle back into his life.

During this time, I developed a closer relationship with my grandparents. After work I would arrive to pick up Megan, and Grandma and Grandpa would insist that I stay for dinner. I enjoyed their company. I learned so much from the two of them about raising children. They were so patient and kind, and Megan was just their little angel.

Still a Mystery

After Megan's birth, Neil and I settled down a bit in our relationship. We sold the trailer and moved in with my mom and dad while we were waiting for our first home to be built. We qualified for a mortgage under a first-time homebuyers' program and worked hard painting and doing some of the work to keep our costs down. Dad was wonderful. He worked as hard as we did on our home. Times weren't bad while we lived with my parents, but it was a good thing when we finally moved into our new home.

Neil played football in the fall, attended school, and worked part time when he could. I continued to work full time, sang in a band on the weekends, and watched my precious little girl grow and change right before my very eyes. I felt sorry for Neil, because with his schedule, he missed so much of Megan's growing up.

Neil was still a mystery to me. I tried and tried to figure him out. I even tried to figure me out, and that was the biggest mystery of all. I was becoming a person I didn't want to be, and I was living a life I didn't want to live. I had always thought that my marriage would be like my mom and dad's marriage. I had such a fine example to follow, yet my life didn't even remotely resemble that example.

I struggled with my feelings for Neil. One minute I loved him with such intensity that I couldn't bear to be without him, and the next minute I despised him. I was like a light switch: on and off, hot and cold. I confused him, and I began to hate myself because of it. I used my mom and dad and my little girl as my retreat. I could hide for days in the same house with Neil, and he didn't even recognize the fact that I was somewhere else emotionally. There were endless nights when I cried myself to sleep, only to wake in the middle of the night with a hopelessness smothering me. He didn't know. Most times he wasn't there.

It was in this period of my life that I began to develop a sleep disorder. I became an insomniac. When I couldn't sleep, I would slip quietly from my bed and spend the hours till dawn cleaning. I had the cleanest, most organized house in the neighborhood. I cleaned cupboards and closets, I dusted and scrubbed, and I vacuumed and did laundry daily. I became fanatical. In between the cleaning frenzies, I worked on crafts, read books, and watched movies. Slowly I slipped further away from Neil. I found myself bobbing in a lake of despair, searching for a vision and asking for a blessing.

Since my withdrawal from college, Grandma Clark and Mom constantly encouraged me to finish. Grandma even said that she would help financially. I was at a point in my life where needed a life preserver. With our relationship struggling, I was surprised to find that Neil supported my decision to go back to school. He knew that it would be a strain on me to spend time away from Megan, but he was willing to try a more active role in parenting. I enrolled in Carroll College's nursing program and started school in the fall of 1980. I was thrilled to be back in a learning environment.

School was difficult. The head of the nursing department had no sympathy or admiration for those students with small children or families. She made it very clear that if you fell behind for any reason, you were out! Some of my peers and I discussed the fact that she must have tortured kittens in her spare time. She was evil, but even though the work was hard, I was doing well.

One evening, Neil came home and informed me that we were moving to Missoula. I stood gaping in horror at the words that escaped his mouth. He had made the decision to move to Missoula without even consulting me! He had a friend who owned a restaurant and had agreed to begin a franchise in Missoula. I didn't want to move—I wanted to finish my schooling, and I was frightened to leave the protective walls that I had built in Helena. I dug in my heels and stayed behind in Helena while he went to Missoula. We saw each other on the weekends, but when that just didn't work, we decided to sell our home and make the move. My lake of despair was now becoming an ocean, and my ship was being tossed upon the rocks, with no lighthouse leading the way. I was drowning.

Before we had a buyer, we moved to Missoula and bought a home there. Neil's business was launched, but it was stifled because of city ordinances and a teachers' strike. Most of our business was kids from the high school across the street, so the strike was devastating to our cash flow. I got a job, and I traveled back to Helena on the weekends to sing with a band. The trouble with my sleep habits only became worse.

Neil and I were slipping further away from each other, and our marriage remained adrift in deep waters. We fought and we made up. Our relationship was so passionate, our arguments intense. We just couldn't get along, but the thought of leaving was terrifying for both of us.

We soon discussed having another child. What were we thinking? Well, regardless of the fact that Neil and I were screwed up, we loved Megan very much. I guess we just thought that maybe a second baby would keep us together.

We never anticipated that we would have such difficulty conceiving. After months of trying with no results, we consulted a doctor. I was prescribed Clomid, a fertility drug. Ironic, isn't it! One month later I was pregnant, and the morning sickness started.

Neil interviewed with a restaurant chain that was opening up a store in Missoula; he was offered a position, and he accepted. I was happy for him, until he broke the news that his manager training was in Kalispell, Montana, which was one hundred twenty-two miles north of Missoula. I was working at the time and was carrying our only health insurance. We just could not afford to lose the insurance with a baby on the way. Consequently, we were living apart again, only this time I was left to take care of a household and a child while working full time. I was an emotional, pregnant wreck. He sometimes had time off on weekends but not always. The baby grew inside me, and I grew cold and more distant. I can't explain the feelings I experienced. I was so confused.

Before the birth, Neil returned to Missoula as manager of the new restaurant. He also coached football at one of the local high schools.

The day before the baby arrived, there was an out-of-town football game. Neil had remained behind only because I had pleaded with him to stay. That day, while shopping, I began early labor. The pains were irregular, but I knew that they were significant. Exhausted, I went to bed about ten o'clock, but I was awakened around midnight with intense pain. I waited until about two thirty in the morning before I woke Neil to go to the hospital. While I was getting Megan up, Neil proceeded to put up a towel bar in the bathroom, one that I had asked him to put up weeks earlier. Funny what stress can make one do!

Lauren Elizabeth Campbell was born September 11, 1983 at 8:34 in the morning. She was smaller than Megan at birth, weighing six pounds, eight and a half ounces. My delivery with Lauren was easier than with Megan, probably because I knew what to expect. Lauren Elizabeth was beautiful, a tiny angel and another gift from God. She had bright red fuzz on her head and big blue eyes.

She was Megan's special baby sister. Megan wanted to do everything for her. She showered Lauren with hugs and kisses and taught her all kinds of things. A bond was established between Megan and her little sister that would be forever true. They grew up together and became the best of friends. Still today their love and admiration for each other is amazing!

The Hurt

In 1986 Neil and I chose to separate. In 1988, after almost two years of separation, we dissolved our eight years of marriage. I ached with the death of our hopes and dreams. I was alone and scared. There had been many battles, and both of us wore the scars of our indifference. We had two beautiful children together, and neither one of us knew exactly how we would handle the painful encounters we knew would be inevitable. Our promise to our girls was that we would always be their mom and dad. Our promise to ourselves was that we would be civil to each other and that we would refrain from quarreling in front of the children.

In the process of our divorce, I received plenty of unsolicited advice from friends. Many of them were trying to be helpful. Most of my friends were also Neil's friends, and our divorce was hard on them, as well. Friends forecast angry disputes, arguments, and resentment between us. I remember speaking with a dear friend, Yvonne Schaff, who had gone through a recent divorce.

"It will be over soon, but don't get your hopes up—it will never really be over!" she stated.

"What?" I questioned. "*What* will never be over?"

"The fighting," Yvonne explained.

"I'm not sure I understand what you mean," I said, perplexed.

"Well, I've heard you say that you think you guys are going to remain friends. I'm here to tell you, it's not going to work out that way. Never! It isn't going to happen. Accept it," she exclaimed.

Reassuringly I stated, "But we've talked about it. We've discussed it. We have agreed that the girls are far too important for us to bicker and argue about every little thing. We will remain friends. I just know it."

Raising her eyebrows, she uttered, "You're dreaming. Look at my ex and me. He can't even stand to be in the same room as me. What does that tell you?"

"I'm not you. This will be different. You'll see. I don't know how to explain it to you, and I'm not expecting you to understand. We have a mutual respect for one another. I love his family, and he loves mine. It's just going to be different," I assured her.

"Well," she advised, "when it all blows up in your face, don't tell me your sad, sad story."

Snapping back, I replied, "I won't have to. Look, I know you are just trying to prepare me for the rocky road ahead. Neil and I may not be friends right now, but I believe we will be."

She mumbled, "Well, if you are, it'll be history in the making."

Eighteen Wheels

Not long after Neil and I separated, I took a job working for a long-haul trucking company. This period in my life was by far the most challenging for me. I was struggling financially, physically, and emotionally. Neil chose to be a somewhat absent father and was absolutely no help to me in raising the girls. I felt as though I had no one in my corner. Sure, family was always just a phone call away, but I was just too damned proud to ask for help. I must have done a good job of disguising my predicament, because no one asked whether I needed help or could use a hand. I was barely scraping by, even working at my job and singing with a band.

I had no other options but to get some help through government assistance. At the grocery store, I was embarrassed to be seen using food stamps by anyone I knew, so I would bundle up my little girls and take them on an adventure in the middle of the night, to the twenty-four-hour grocery store. At least we had food on our table. I also received assistance on my power bill, so we stayed warm in our little apartment. I vowed that as soon as I was on my feet, I would get off assistance.

At the trucking company, I manned the reception desk, worked as a secretary, and answered phones. On a daily basis, I spoke with all of the drivers and connected them to dispatch. I quickly learned their names and recognized their voices. I was interested in their chosen profession and was somewhat envious of their travels throughout the United States and Canada. I'd have given anything to have been able to pack up my little girls and venture to someplace new.

Early one morning, I answered the phone with a friendly "Good morning." The voice on the other end was unfamiliar.

"Hi, ma'am. I need to speak with dispatch."

"And you are?"

"My name's Ryne Brockway. I'm the guy who owns truck unit number 276."

"Oh," I exclaimed. "I haven't talked to you before, have I?"

"No," he replied. "I had a driver on my truck because I was taking care of some personal business, but I'm back driving now, so I'll be callin' in every day."

"Okay, Ryne," I said. "My name's Becky, and it's nice to meet you. Have a great day!"

I looked on the roster and saw that he was a Canadian owner/operator. Although he pronounced his name Ryan, it was spelled differently. I questioned my co-worker about him, but she didn't really know much. He had a really nice voice, and I just wanted to know a little bit about him, so I checked out his file. I discovered that he was younger than the others drivers of the fleet, but there was no photo, so I had no face to connect with his voice.

Over the course of the next several weeks we developed a comfortable rapport. His calls came from all over the United States and Canada as he drove from one destination to the next. He would often call in several times a day to talk to dispatch, and I found myself anxiously anticipating his calls.

I discovered a lot about him in those brief exchanges. I learned that he was married with two small children, a daughter and son. I told him about my sweet little girls and revealed that I was separated from my husband and was having a bit of a difficult time. He offered me comforting words of encouragement. Although cautious, I felt somewhat safe in opening up to him. After all, he was married and was always hundreds of miles away.

The awards banquet for the company was an annual event that was long awaited by the employees and the owner/operators. Most of them would make the trip to Missoula for the dinner and the festivities. It was held around the holiday season, and I was delighted to learn that I would finally meet Ryne face to face.

A co-worker had asked me to accompany him to the dinner, and I discovered that I was rather nervous as I dressed for my night out. Little Megan and Lauren sat on the edge of the bed and giggled as I slipped into my black party dress. They were always a source of comfort and support for me. They told me I looked beautiful and helped me decide what jewelry I should wear. I promised to kiss them when I got home. My date arrived, and I said good-bye to the girls and the babysitter.

When we arrived at the hotel, the happy hour was well under way. My date asked if I would like a cocktail, and I nodded a yes. I stood all by myself as I looked around the room for a familiar face. Wringing my hands in silent desperation, I asked myself what in the world I was doing there. As I searched for an empty chair, I felt like a fish out of water. Spotting a safe spot for retreat, I took a step in that direction. From behind me, a soft, kind voice uttered, "Surely this has got to be Becky." I turned to see a handsome young man with a grin and an outstretched hand. It was Ryne.

Standing next to him, looking quite perplexed, was his wife, Niki. Her arms were crossed in front of her, and I could tell that she was no more comfortable there than I was. We quickly exchanged hellos, and then Ryne asked if there was room for him and Niki to sit at our table.

I smiled and said, "We just got here and haven't found a place to sit just yet." Ryne surveyed the room and motioned for me to follow. He had spotted four empty seats at a nearby table. He quickly pulled out a chair for his wife, and as she sat down, he gestured for me to take the seat next to him. Respectfully he introduced himself and Niki to those already seated at the table. She nodded at each person as her eyes moved around the table. It might have been just my perception, mind you, but when her eyes fell on me, they felt like hot pokers searing my brain. She grimaced and quickly looked away.

My date arrived at the table and handed me a glass of wine. My hands were trembling as I lifted the glass to my mouth and took a gulp. I recognized several of the guys at the table, and it wasn't long before the men were all engaging in friendly conversation. Quietly, I tried to gain my composure, but I just couldn't stop shaking. I dug in my purse for my cigarettes. Placing one in my lips, I tried to light it, but somehow, I could not gain control of my shaking hand. In a flash, my date and Ryne commenced a friendly competition to aid me in my quest for fire. Being closer, my date won the contest, and Ryne smiled as he dropped his lighter back on the table in front of his wife.

I relaxed a bit after dinner was served, making pleasant conversation with Ryne and Niki. When the music started, Ryne inquired if I would like to dance with him. I reluctantly accepted his invitation as I caught a glare from his wife. When the song finished, I declined a second dance with him and returned to the table.

The night's events came to a conclusion, but not before Ryne and I had solidified our friendship. It was nice to finally have connected Ryne's gentle voice with his face. He quietly apologized for Niki's cold reception and assured me that she was just shy and not comfortable around strangers.

"Liar," I thought. She just didn't like me; that was evident. I guess I really couldn't blame her. After all, I probably talked to her husband more than she did in any given day. We said good night as I left the room with my date.

Over the next several months, Ryne and I became good friends. We always had a short, personal exchange of conversation before I transferred him to dispatch. I got to know him very well and could sense in his voice whether his day was going well or not. He teased me and always inquired about my daughters and what was happening in my life.

Picking up the phone one afternoon, I was concerned at how anxious Ryne sounded. I asked him what was wrong, but he declined explanation. He said that it was not a good time for him to discuss it. I offered support for whatever was bothering him, and he asked if he could call me at home that evening. This was stepping over the boundaries for me, and I was reluctant, but I could sense that he really needed a friend to talk to. I gave him my home phone number. All afternoon I worried about him. He was such a nice guy. What could possibly be bothering him?

The call came late that night. The operator on the other end of the line asked if I was willing to accept charges from Ryne. I was surprised that he would call collect, but I accepted.

The first words out of his mouth were, "Hi, sorry I have to charge this to you, but I don't have a credit card. Is that okay? I mean, I will pay you for the call. I don't expect you to pay for it." He sounded unstrung and exhausted.

"What is wrong? Are you okay?" I questioned.

"It's my marriage, Beck." My heart fell to the floor.

"Ryne, I am so sorry. What happened?"

Niki wanted a separation, and he was devastated! I listened well into the night as he spoke of difficult times in his relationship. He was sad and confused. I knew all too well how he felt. My life was still shattered, and picking up the pieces had been a slow and painful process. I tried to console him, and he thanked me for my discerning ear and words of wisdom. I bid him a good night and hung up the phone.

My heart was breaking for this young man and his situation. Consequently, I began to forget about my dilemma as I counseled him and validated his feelings. I encouraged him to convince Niki to seek the help of a professional marriage counselor. He said she would not agree to do so. He was an emotional wreck. I was concerned for him but was relieved when he told me that he would not do anything foolish, like take to drinking in an effort to drown his sorrows.

After weeks of uncertainty, he and Niki finally settled on a separation. She wanted to go back to Quebec, where her family was, and he agreed to take her there. He loaded up their household and his two little children and drove them there. He helped her get situated, kissed his babies good bye, and headed west.

I felt pain in my heart for him. He was such a kind and gentle man, and I wanted to be his strength to get him through this. We talked almost every night; my phone bills were huge. He was true to his word and paid them. He needed to hear my voice on the other end of the phone whenever he could. I became his refuge.

Almost two years had passed since our first hello. We had become dear friends over the phone lines. He was my sounding board and I his. We were alike in so many ways. We had similar backgrounds, and we were both looking for the same thing: a lasting relationship with someone who would love us unconditionally.

Meet Me in Montana

It was late on a Wednesday afternoon, and he was somewhere outside Austin, Texas, when I got his call. As usual, his mood was quite upbeat.

"Howdy, ma'am!" this voice drawled.

I laughed as I recognized his unmistakable voice. "Yeah, cowboy, whadda ya want?" I posed.

"You," was his simple response.

Shocked, I waited for something to come out of my mouth. What was I to say to that? At my loss for words, he interrupted the silence.

"Becky, will you agree to meet me in Great Falls? I want to see you. Here's the deal. I will drive straight through to Montana to be there late Saturday night. Can you make it?"

I stuttered and searched for an answer. "Well, Ryne, I don't know what to say! Can I think about it? I'm caught a little off guard here."

"Of course. I don't want to pressure you, but please consider it. I'll talk to you later tonight."

That evening I asked one of my friends, Noel, for some advice. I wanted someone to tell me what to do. Noel simply looked at me with disbelief as she spouted, "What's to think about? He's so sweet, and you guys have been talking on the phone for over a year now. I think you should go. I'll even take care of the girls for you."

I had never done this sort of thing before in my life. I was going to drive over one hundred miles, in a car that was unpredictable, after playing all night with the band. It would be late at night, on an unfamiliar highway, and I would be driving all by myself to meet a truck driver in a truck stop? Had I lost it? Surely there was something terribly wrong with this picture.

I was a bundle of nerves when his evening phone call finally came. I could feel his apprehension about my decision, and I couldn't tell whether it was relief or fear he felt when I finally answered yes.

He cautioned me to be careful on the drive. "Watch for deer along that highway. Don't stop on the road, and don't talk to strangers." They were gentle reminders that he cared about my safety. He continued with instruction. "I'll be arriving before you. If you decide not to come, please just leave a message for me at the fuel desk. If you do come, look for my semi parked with the other trucks. I'll probably be asleep, so just knock on the driver's door. I sleep pretty sound, so knock hard."

I safely filed his instructions in my mind and prepared for my adventure. I made arrangements for the girls to stay with my friend, and I made up some story for my family as to where I was going for this 1988 Memorial Day weekend.

I watched the clock slowly tick away the minutes during my band's gig. When the last break was over, it was about twelve thirty in the morning. There was only one more set, and then I would be on my way. I knew I would need caffeine in my system for the long drive ahead, so I gulped back a

Coke. The guys in the band had agreed to tear down the equipment without me—only because they knew I would be driving to Great Falls that night. It was shortly before one thirty in the morning when we concluded our last song. I ran to the restroom and quickly changed my clothes.

I stopped at a convenience store and purchased a six-pack of Mountain Dew, the highest-caffeine-content drink available. I fueled my car, checked the oil, kicked the tires, and washed the windshield. I pulled onto the interstate shortly after two o'clock. I rounded a bend and the lights of Missoula disappeared from my view. I was alone in the dark, speeding toward an uncertain rendezvous.

I drank soda, smoked cigarettes, and drove with the window down to help keep me awake. It wasn't long before the effects of too much liquid and too much caffeine came over me. I had to pee, and I remembered Ryne had instructed me not to stop or pull off the road—but golly, my bladder was screaming at me!

My car was an old, unpredictable piece of junk. Sometimes it just wouldn't start even if it had been running fine all day. A mechanic had told me that the starter was wearing out, but I couldn't afford to fix it, so I babied it. Ryne would have been furious with me if he had known there was a problem with my car and I hadn't told him.

I pulled off the highway and carefully placed my handbag over the accelerator pedal. The engine revved, piercing the silence of the forest outside. I crawled across the front seat and opened the passenger door. It was pitch-black out. The moon was hidden behind a cloud, and the only light in the dark was streaming from my headlights. I quickly dropped my pants and squatted. I sighed with relief as I pulled up my trousers and climbed back in the car. I locked the door behind me and slipped my foot under my handbag. I went on.

With every mile I watched for deer along the roadside, but I certainly didn't see the owl coming as he swooped from the trees and hit the left side of my windshield. He bounced across the hood of the car and then flew off into the night. I was startled and quite shaken by the event. I felt awful that I had hit him, but angry that he had cracked my windshield. I continued down the road, once again scanning the borrow pit for creatures just waiting to jump out in front of my car. It was a long trip, and I sang at the top of my voice for comfort as I slugged down the last of my sodas.

The highway sign said Great Falls 4 Miles. I began to feel queasy. What if he wasn't there? What if he hadn't made it? Oh God, what if he was there? What if he *had* made it? I took the appropriate exit from the highway and turned the car. Up ahead, a neon sign read Truck Stop, Open 24 Hours. I slowly steered my car into the parking lot. Semis were parked side by side, and I could hear the sound of idling engines and smell the odor of diesel fumes. My tired eyes searched the rows of trucks, and soon I spotted the number 279 on a front fender.

I parked in front of the restaurant and turned off my engine. I sat there and stared forward for a few minutes before I grabbed my handbag and climbed out of my car. The door slammed behind me as I looked around the lot. The restaurant was open, so I went inside to use the ladies' room. When I entered the restaurant, a waitress smiled and pointed in the direction of the restroom. I turned on the light and looked at my tired image in the mirror. I brushed my teeth, brushed my hair, and splashed cold water on my face. After refreshing my makeup, I took a deep breath and turned out the light.

The hum of the engines was deafening as I made my way down the row of trucks to Ryne's door. Reaching to the handle for support, I pulled myself up on the high step. I tapped lightly on the window and then waited. No sound or movement came from inside the cab. I tapped again, a little louder this time, and peered in the window. The curtain covering the sleeper moved and my heart beat faster, but there was still no sign of him. I finally knocked louder, and Ryne pulled back the curtain and jumped from his bed.

Still peering in the window, I quickly looked away, because I saw that he was standing in his underwear. His eyes searched the dimly lit lot through his windshield. Suddenly he grabbed for a blanket and wrapped it hurriedly around his body. His head turned to me, staring at him through the window. He shook his head and reached for the door handle.

A smile came over his face as his voice cracked with, "Hello there. Well, come on in and shut the door." He motioned for me to sit as he sat of the edge of his bed.

I sat down in the driver seat and turned to face him. "Hi," I said. "I'm here."

"Yes, you are. Indeed, you are," he said quietly as his hand reached for an envelope sitting on the console. He handed it to me. I opened it and read the words inscribed: "When this card arrives, you'll know it's from my heart. Wishing we were inches instead of miles apart. To a very special lady. Love, Ryne." I smiled as he then handed me a small statue of a Texas armadillo. I thanked him and listened as he began to speak.

"When I got here, I checked at the fuel desk. I kind of figured there would be a message from you that you weren't coming. You see, I knew you were too much of a lady to meet a rogue like me in a truck stop—but you were too much of a lady to stand me up without leaving me a message too. When there wasn't a note from you, I knew you'd show. But, now that you're here, I don't quite know what to say. Are you hungry?" he questioned.

I answered yes, not knowing what else to say.

He smiled and said, "Let me get some clothes on, and we'll go on into the restaurant and I'll feed ya."

"Okay," I responded. I was relieved to leave the confines of the cab of his semi.

The waitress smiled as she took our order. We filled the next few minutes with small talk as we sipped our coffee. Our food arrived, and I watched as he devoured pork chops and gravy with hash browns and toast. He kept asking me if I was okay as I picked at my food. Truth was, I was nervous as hell and didn't have much of an appetite.

He looked different than I had remembered him from the Christmas party. He was quite thin and had longer hair than before. The dark circles under his eyes told me he was tired, but his face lit up and he laughed as I told him about my drive.

His smile was warm as he reached across the table and rested his hand on mine. "Thank you for coming. You have no idea what this means to me. I have thought of nothing else but you since leaving Texas. It's so good to see you again."

After hours of conversation, I tried to suppress a yawn but couldn't, and we soon agreed that sleep would do us both good. I was apprehensive as we crawled inside his cab and terrified when he motioned for me to lie beside him. We lay next to each other in the dark, and soon my eyes closed and my breathing became more relaxed. He held me as I drifted off to sleep and then he, too, fell asleep.

We were awakened by engines throttling up as truckers moved their big rigs from their slumber. It was chaotic and noisy outside as trucks began to leave. Ryne pulled me close and we both fell back to sleep as the racket diminished.

We slept until early afternoon and as the sun climbed higher in the sky, the temperature inside the cab began to rise. Ryne's air conditioner in his truck wasn't working and it became very unpleasant.

With some reservation, we agreed to get a motel room. I knew we would be more comfortable, but I had never done that sort of thing before, and it made me very nervous. I sat in my car as he ran in to get the room. I was even concerned that there would be raised eyebrows from the person at the check-in desk. They probably could have cared less, but I felt awkward. We pulled up to the room, and Ryne came around to open the car door for me. He reached out his hand for mine, and we smiled at each other as he pulled me to my feet. He made me feel so giddy; I hoped he couldn't see how my knees were shaking as he turned the key in the lock.

We turned on the television and he flipped through the channels. We had our choice of racing, bowling, or golf. We kicked off our shoes and climbed up on the bed, propping the pillows behind our heads. Lying close to one another, we talked for hours, laughing and giggling as we shared secrets, stories, and pizza. I dozed off to sleep again, only to be awakened with a gentle kiss.

The kiss turned to passion, and we embraced, our bodies melting together with a sudden longing. We spent the entire day in that motel room. We shared love, and we laughed, and we listened to one another's stories of childhood and heartbreak. Our day together was extraordinary. At the close of the day, I had to leave and drive back home to Missoula. It was difficult to say good-bye to him. He kissed me sweetly and tenderly and told me to drive safely. I watched him in the rearview mirror as he waved. I hoped that when tomorrow came I would be able to discern what this feeling was. Was it merely lust, or was it love?

We met many times after that, and we wrote long letters to each other. Our exchanges revealed our innermost thoughts. He was a sensitive individual, and I longed for a deeper understanding of just what made him tick. I found myself wanting to be near him more and more. I felt complete when I was with him. He was gentle and caring, and I was thankful he was in my life.

He says he fell in love with me in that motel room in Great Falls on that hot Memorial Day in 1988. I don't know when it happened for me. Maybe it was before that day. Maybe it was during one of our long telephone conversations. Maybe I fell in love with him as I read his carefully worded letters, or it could have happened when he filled my grocery cart and then gladly paid the bill. I don't really know. All I know is that I had fallen in love all over again.

My sweetheart, Ryne and me in 1989

Painful Memories

I was still working at the trucking company when the girls and I moved to a very cute little apartment that was owned by my mom's brother. It was more like a home than any place we had lived since Neil and I had separated. My uncle allowed me to paint and do a little fixing up. He knew that I would take care of the place, and he was delighted to have us there. Lauren and Megan loved it! We had a little backyard, and there was a babbling brook that ran behind the house. I had humble furnishings, but it was clean and comfortable and close to Megan's school and my work.

Neil and I had tried reconciliation and had gone to counseling, but there was no hope for putting our marriage back together. It seemed that almost every night, after I put my girls to bed, I would cry. I was so lonely and certain that I would be for the rest of my life.

It was the week of Christmas, 1987. I had talked to my parents earlier in the week. After the first of the year, Daddy needed to have some minor surgery on his elbow to remove a bone spur that was giving him some discomfort. Because of his age and the fact that he was a smoker, his doctor wanted to get a chest x-ray before the surgery to make sure that everything looked good. I told Mom to get back to me and let me know when the surgery was scheduled.

She called the day after the x-ray with some disturbing news. The doctor had detected a dark spot on one of Daddy's lungs. He said there was really no way to be certain what it was until he did a biopsy, and that was to happen January 1. I was worried and anxiously waited for the results of the biopsy.

It was the following Wednesday night when I got the phone call from Mom. I could hear fear in her voice as she began to speak. "Beck, I have some bad news. We have the results of the biopsy, and the spot they saw in the x-ray is cancer; your daddy has cancer in his lung." Those words were so hard for my mom to convey. Her voice was shaking, and I could tell that she had been crying.

It all happened so fast! He was scheduled for surgery to remove the portion of his lung that had the tumor. His physician felt confident that he could remove the entire tumor and then follow up with successful radiation. Daddy's doctor explained that most lung cancers were not found in time to treat, and most were inoperable. At least they had detected the cancer early enough to operate. That was encouraging.

Daddy's surgery was scheduled the day of their thirty-seventh wedding anniversary. They agreed that it had always been a special day for them, so what better day could there possibly be to face something as vitally important as this surgery? They were both so brave. Deb, Pam, Phil, and I sat and waited with Mom in the waiting room. The hours went by slowly. When the doctor finally appeared, he said that everything had gone well and he felt the surgery had been successful. They would be sending tissue samples off to the pathology lab to determine whether they had been able to get all of the cancer cells. We could only hope and pray that the results would be favorable.

Daddy had a long recovery; progress was slow and laborious. He was given the best of care after his surgery—by the team of nurses and by all of us, especially Phil. Even the nurses commented on how attentive my brother was with him. Daddy had a breathing tube in for the first twenty-four hours, and soon after that was removed, we were able to speak with him. He was so courageous!

His lung capacity was much diminished, because they had removed a large quadrant of his lung. He had to blow into a bladder device to exercise his lung. His recovery was painful and difficult for him, but he had such a great attitude, and he and Mom were bound and determined to beat the cancer. All of us were supportive and kept in close contact with Mom and Dad during that most difficult period.

Daddy had to go to Great Falls for radiation treatments. Mom was still working, and every day that he traveled to Great Falls in the hospital van she wished she could be with him. I'm sure this was a factor in her taking an early retirement from the company she worked for. After Dad's last radiation treatment, my mom and dad decided they would take a much-needed trip. They went to see Mom's brother and sister-in-law on the West Coast. They both had worked so hard their entire lives, and it seemed so unfair that at this juncture in their lives they were faced with such a frightening illness.

Daddy was exhausted and had lost his appetite. Eating had always been one of his simple pleasures in life, but after the radiation, everything he ate tasted metallic. The doctor said that it was from the treatments. Daddy was also in constant pain, each and every day. It had been a difficult year so far for him. Mom worried about him, but she didn't seek us out for support. She stuffed her fears and carried the burden of worry herself.

On March 25, 1988, the day before my thirty-first birthday, Grandpa Walt died. He had spent the latter part of his life at a nursing home. My grandpa, Walter Leslie Clark, had been ninety-seven years old, and his death was bittersweet. He had been angry that God had made him live so long. His mind had been clear but his body had become aged and worn out. We hated to see him leave, but we rejoiced to know he was no longer suffering.

I moved from Missoula to Helena in July 1988 so that I could be closer to Mom and Dad. Something told me that the following months would be crucial and I just couldn't afford to miss this time. I spent every bit of time that I possibly could with my dad. I clung to his every word, knowing our time together was precious. I watched as Mom grew distant, her every thought and concern focused on Dad. She was edgy and became less and less tolerant of my visits to see Dad. I was made to feel that I was intruding on her time with Daddy, her lifelong companion. She acted as if I were being selfish. I tried to put this into perspective, but sometimes it was pretty difficult to do so. I knew that she and Dad had kept many of the difficult times from us, and I also knew that she believed my daddy's remaining time was short.

In February 1989, Grandma Clark was diagnosed with colon cancer. By the time it was discovered, the cancer was inoperable and the prognosis grim. She wasn't terribly sick in the beginning, but the cancer grew quickly and her frail little body struggled to fight back. Daddy tried to see Grandma as often as he could, but he was sick himself, and traveling the thirty-three miles to see her was nearly impossible. I tried to see my grandma every weekend, and I spent as many weekday evenings as possible with my dad.

Dad and Grandma were both battling cancer, and my mom was battling depression, anger, fear, and anxiety. Watching Grandma slip away and dealing with Daddy's illness was taking its toll on her. She began to share her fears that Daddy was getting sicker, getting worse. You could see it on her face and hear it in her voice as she spoke. She and Daddy were so devoted to one another; they were inseparable. They both knew the cancer had returned, even before the doctor confirmed it.

It was the spring of 1989 when Daddy's cancer did once again ignite, and this time it attacked with a vengeance. The doctors struck it aggressively with more radiation, but Daddy was in greater danger this time. The cancer had eaten through his esophagus, and he was soon hospitalized and a feeding tube inserted. The fact that Daddy would never again be able eat was terrifying.

I remember going to see him in the hospital and trying so hard to cheer him. To the contrary, he actually always made *me* feel better. He had accepted his fate and wanted to make each remaining minute of his life count. One day, after work, I went to see him at the hospital. I was wearing a bright salmon-colored dress I had just purchased. Daddy was so serious when he smiled and asked me to do him a favor and stand on one leg.

I looked at him, puzzled, but I obliged. So, there I was, standing on one leg at the end of his bed, when a nurse entered the room and asked, "Kenny, what are you up to in here?"

"Well," he answered, "I'm thinking my daughter looks just like a pink flamingo. Whadda *you* think?"

I smiled as we all broke into laughter. Mom always did say that Dad was near perfect, except for the fact that he loved those crazy, tacky pink flamingo lawn ornaments! He was so ill, but he still had his endearing sense of humor and his passion for life.

Although there were only a few miles distance between mother and son, the cancer continued to prevent my dad and my grandma from visiting one another. They spoke on the phone, talking of the bygone days and encouraging one another. It tore our hearts out to see them both enduring such pain and suffering.

Our prayers for a miracle cure diminished, and we began to pray that Daddy would become stable enough to leave the hospital and return home to die. Our prayers for Grandma were that the Lord would be swift and take her.

Bringing Daddy home was a fulfillment of his request to die at home, on his mountain. When the day finally came that the doctor believed he was stable enough to be transferred home, preparations were made to accommodate him, and hospice was called in to assist our family.

Hospice is an organization that provides round-the-clock care for the dying, and they administer support to the family members as they prepare for the death of loved ones. Ironically, my dear, sweet Jim Reeves was instrumental in establishing hospice care in Helena.

Mom wasn't quite ready to give Daddy's care up to hospice, but she resigned herself to the fact that she couldn't handle his care alone. We had a great deal of family who had gathered to support my mom and dad in this difficult time. Daddy's sisters were both in Montana, taking turns caring for Grandma and Dad, and Mom's brothers and their wives were also there.

Looking back on my daddy's last hours, what I remember is the confusion and the anxiety, the smell of cancer, and the sound of the oxygen pump. Ryne was with me during this time. He explained to me that he didn't think he had ever really grieved the loss of his own father, so he experienced this difficult transition right along with me. I never would have made it through those horrible hours without him.

The morning before Daddy's passing was beautiful on his mountain. He wanted his fingernails clipped and filed, so Mom asked if I would do that for him. I sat close to him and held his hand in mine. His nerve endings were so sensitive that it was very uncomfortable for him to even be touched. He was apprehensive to even communicate that to me, because he loved me so. Tears filled his eyes as we spoke of his inevitable death, but he was not afraid. He believed that soon he would be with the Lord and that he would no longer feel the pain of the cancer consuming his very breath. With great difficulty, he spoke to me of one grave concern.

"Beck, you kids need to be patient with your mom. She is going to need your love and support like never before. You don't know her as well as I know her. Please remember patience." His blue eyes were weary and his speech was broken as those words departed his lips. With all his strength, he squeezed my hand and smiled as Mom entered the room.

I stood, kissed his forehead, and whispered, "I love you." His eyes followed me as I left the room and closed the door behind me. It wasn't long after that that the hospice nurse emerged from the bedroom and told all of us that Momma and Daddy needed some time alone.

An hour or so later, Mom entered the living room and quietly sat on the sofa. She stared out the window and slowly spoke. "Your daddy, our precious Ken, is ready to die. He has been holding on because he is worried about all of us, especially me. I told him it's okay to go. I told him it's okay to go." The room was awkwardly silent.

Later that afternoon, Daddy lost his ability to speak. His brain was not receiving enough oxygen to keep him lucid, and more morphine was administered to keep him comfortable.

His doctor visited Daddy, and the family gathered in the living room as he explained, "It won't be long. Ken is in the last stage of his life. It is important for you to know that he can still hear you, but it won't be long now." He went on to further explain that Daddy's lungs were filling with fluid, and he reassured us that he was not experiencing pain.

Night fell on the saddened mountain, and thousands of stars wept in the Montana sky as a hush enveloped the house. I was exhausted, having not slept in days. Ryne and I crawled onto the bed in one of the downstairs bedrooms. I was lulled to sleep by the sound of the oxygen pump coming from the upstairs bedroom, where my mom clung to Daddy for the very last time.

Morning erupted with a knock at the bedroom door. It was my aunt. Her voice quivered as she spoke through the closed door. "Beck, your daddy's leaving. It's time."

I jumped to the floor and squeezed Ryne's hand as I headed for the stairs. Looking back, I said, "Ryne, I need you. Please be with me now."

By the time I entered the bedroom, Mom, Deb, Pam, and Phil were already there. Many other family members were gathered in the living room and in the hall. Phil motioned for me to kneel next to him. Ryne waited outside with the rest of my family. There we prayed the Lord's Prayer as our beloved father, brother, husband, and friend left this world to be with our Lord. It was peaceful as we watched the last breath leave his lips. Kenneth Philip Clark, a great man, my daddy, ascended into heaven on May 25, 1989.

The next morning, I took Mom to Townsend. We drove in silence, knowing what we must now face. It was early as we walked up the steps to Grandma's back door. Daddy's sisters met us at the door, and we hugged each other as we stepped inside.

"How is she?" Mom asked.

"It's bad, Betts," my aunt said. Screams came from the bedroom where my tiny little grandma writhed in pain. Mom entered the room, and I watched as she climbed onto the bed next to Grandma.

Holding my grandma close, Momma whispered in her ear. "Verna—Mom—it's me, Betty. I've come to see tell you something. Ken is gone, Verna. He is with God now. Do you understand what I've said?"

Grandma's frail little body quieted with my momma's words, and she began to cry. I held onto Grandma's hand as Momma rocked her, saying, "I know, Verna, I know. It's okay, it's okay."

My eyes met Momma's, and I could tell that she was about to break down. She needed to leave the room. "It's okay, Mom. I'll stay with her." It was the last time I sang to my grandma. She sobbed like a child as my voice carried to her ears the words and melodies of her most treasured hymns. I left the room as my aunts and Grandma's doctor tried desperately to find a pliant vein to give her more morphine for her intolerable pain.

We kissed Grandma good-bye that afternoon. Verna Price Clark, my beloved grandma, died three long days later, on May 29, 1989, and the angels rejoiced! It was a very bad spring, but apple trees blossomed just the same.

Married, with Children

Ryne and I were married on a snowy afternoon, September 8, 1989, in a small log chapel on the top of McDonald Pass, outside of Helena, Montana. It was an intimate and beautiful ceremony performed by Father Loren Foot, a family friend and an Episcopalian priest. In attendance were Mom, Grandma Smith, Megan, Lauren, and friends, Steve and Yvonne Schaff, who stood up for us.

After the wedding, Ryne and I took everyone out to dinner, and then we drove to Alberta, Canada. We were scheduled to leave the next morning from Calgary to fly to Montreal, Quebec, to finally meet his children, Natashia and Nathan, and go on our honeymoon. Regrettably, I had agreed to take his children with us to Niagara Falls for our trip. I had never met them, and Ryne had only spoken with them over the phone about having someone else in his life, but they certainly didn't know that we were married, nor did his ex-wife. As far as they knew, we were just coming for a visit so they could meet me.

His ex-wife, Niki, and the children picked us up from the airport, and we then drove to their house to get Ryne's pickup truck, which he had left there when he'd moved them to Montreal. I was unaware of the fact that, at the airport, his ex had coldly addressed the issue of our sleeping arrangements while traveling with the children. That was when Ryne had apparently dropped the bomb that we were married and flashed his wedding ring as proof. Consequently, Niki and the children ignored me on the drive to their home. I felt very ill at ease, but there was no immediate way out of the situation, so I just sat there and said nothing.

The children were not quite ready, so we had to wait for them to finish packing. We were invited in, but the atmosphere remained rather awkward. Thank God we didn't have to wait very long, and with the pickup loaded, we were ready for our journey.

Ryne lifted up little Nathan, who was only three years old, and strapped him into a child-restraint seat. Natashia, only five, was given a boost up to sit by her little brother. Ryne carefully strapped her in and told her, "Now, sweetheart, you get to sit by Rebecca, but you need to make Daddy a promise and keep your seatbelt buckled, okay?"

Natashia looked at her daddy and then looked at me as she said, "Well, Daddy, I think that *she* should sit by the door, then Nathan, and then me. I should sit by you. It's just better that way. At least *she* doesn't get to sit by you!"

Ryne looked at me with a shocked look that turned to a smile as I said, "Well, I think that's a great idea. Nathan can sit by me, and you can be your daddy's buddy and sit by him."

Oh, but that was only the beginning. We were no more than a block away, after a *very* long good-bye with their mother, when Natashia folded her little arms tightly and turned to me as she said, "You're not my mom, and I don't have to do anything you say, because my mom said so." Period! Ryne and I caught a glance from each other, and then stared straight ahead as silence fell upon the "happy travelers"!

Thus, our wedding night was spent driving cross-country from Montana to Alberta, and the first night of our honeymoon was spent in the company of two very determined little children.

The first night, we were tired from the drive when we arrived at the motel. With two beds in the room, we figured Nathan and Natashia could sleep in one and we could share the other. Again, Natashia had her own idea, and so it was Ryne and the kids in one bed and me, alone, in the other. I remember thinking to myself, "Wow, Beck! You've managed to have two marriages and two really horrible wedding nights. This has got to be a record!" Where were The Duke and *Big Jake* when I needed them, now?

Our trip was out of the ordinary, to say the least. Yes, we did spend our honeymoon at Niagara Falls, the honeymoon capital of the world, but all I can clearly remember about the trip is that we ate at McDonald's three times a day, trudged around with two children, and I slept alone.

I loved watching the interaction between Ryne and his children. He was so patient and kind and dealt with the entire situation quite calmly. I was the one who was stressed. Nathan and Natashia didn't want anything to do with me, and I wanted so badly for them to accept me and simply give me a chance. It's possible that they had received a bit of counseling with regard to me, from their mother, prior to our meeting—and they were just children, after all.

After our honeymoon trip and the drive back to Montreal to return the children, Ryne and I headed west for a very long drive back to Montana and home.

MARRIED, WITH CHILDREN

*Photo of our wedding
Ryne Brockway and Rebecca C Brockway, Forever
photo with Lauren and Megan*

Photo of all four kiddos
From Left to Right—Natashia Brockway, Nathan Brockway,
Lauren Campbell and Megan Campbell

In Sickness and in Health

Ryne and I established our new life together in Montana. I worked for state government in Helena and Ryne was, of course, still trucking. At times I still felt like a single mom, with Ryne gone so much. We adapted as well as possible to being apart, but I admit that it was difficult. Within a few short weeks of returning home from our honeymoon trip we moved to a different home and I, with a long history of female maladies, began to hemorrhage and had to have an emergency hysterectomy in October, 1989.

At two o'clock on a Monday morning, January 1990, Ryne left our home in Helena, bound for the west coast. He had been home for several days, and on Sunday we had watched the Super Bowl on our recently purchased color television. Sometime between the time Ryne left and Megan's alarm sounding at six thirty, we were robbed. The thieves had entered the house through the back door and had taken the television, the VCR, all the meat from the freezer, and the school lunches I had made for the girls. The bold bandits even helped themselves to the box of "Dove Ice Cream Bars," my confectionary treats! It was frightening to think that strangers had been in our home while the girls and I were sleeping! The police weren't much help and the entire event really traumatized little eleven-year-old Megan. She had a difficult time getting past the fear that the robbery invoked.

It wasn't long before our long-distance marriage took its toll on us both. We missed each other so very much and just wanted to be together. Ryne was soon offered an office job with the trucking company he was leased to, and he jumped at the chance to come off the road. The job was in Missoula, and I was all too happy to return to the town I had grown to love. So, it was off to Missoula once again.

Megan and Lauren loved living in Missoula and dove right into school and making friends. Ryne settled in his new job, and I settled into life again as a working mother and wife. I got a job at the University of Montana, and life was good.

Sometimes my responsibilities as an employee, a wife, and a mother seemed too numerous and overwhelming. I often felt as though I were wandering in a circle, much as a wildebeest does right before it yields to death. Why I felt I had to keep all the plates spinning is beyond my understanding. I even found myself saying things like, "Oh, I need to be busy," or "I operate at my optimum level if I am going in a hundred different directions, anyway." Who was I kidding? I tried to be a super mom and *all* things to everyone *all* of the time. Little did I know I was plummeting; my years of sleep deprivation and my stressful lifestyle would soon entangle.

Ryne recognized this, and for the first time in my life I was offered the freedom of quitting my job and becoming a stay-at-home mom. Ryne's income afforded me the luxury of being more attentive to the needs of my family, and I was able to have some much-needed, well-deserved personal time. I took up scrapbooking, gained some reading mileage, began writing, and honed my gardening skills.

Ryne and I had just successfully completed renovating our home, and we made the decision to sell and buy a brand-new home only a half mile or so from our old home. I accepted the responsibility of preparing our old house for sale and packing to move. There was a great deal of organizing to be done. It's amazing just how much I had gathered in a few short years. I wanted to think of my collection of nonessentials as extensions of my personality, but that was a complete stretch. I had to confront the fact that I just had lots of stuff!

It was spring of 1996, and the move went as smoothly as one could expect. I contracted a nasty respiratory flu, and it soon moved into my chest. I was feverish and weak, not to mention exhausted from the move. I didn't go to the doctor right away, because I thought it was just the flu, but after two months of feeling this way, I decided to see a doctor. Tests revealed nothing more than some congestion in my lungs, which I already suspected, but I was so tired all the time and achy all over my body. I just couldn't get enough sleep!

I wanted to go back to work and started a new job in August. I tried to keep up with everything, but I felt sick every day. I didn't know what was wrong, nor did any doctor, for that matter. I was referred from doctor to doctor, praying that someone could help me. But time after time and test after test, they found nothing conclusive. My body hurt everywhere, and the intensity of pain varied from day to day. I couldn't sleep at night. My digestive system was not functioning properly, and I was always fatigued. My family felt helpless as they all watched me slip deeper into depression. My moods were up and down, and I found that my bad days far outweighed my good days. I tried to keep a positive attitude for my family, friends, and co-workers, but some days that was just impossible. I felt as though I were dying a slow and painful death.

Doctors and professionals raised their eyebrows as I described my symptoms which, quite frankly, painted a bleak picture of my quality of life. Family and friends listened to my tales of frustration, but no one really believed I was sick! I didn't look ill. I had gained weight, so I thought that maybe if I could just lose some weight my spirits would lift and the pain would go away. So, I lost weight, but the pain remained. Every night I closed my eyes and prayed to God that I would awaken to a pain-free morning. It never came.

I was crazy—that was it! I was slowly going insane. That happens sometimes, you know. Something was happening inside my brain. The doctors couldn't find anything wrong with me physically, so I must be crazy!

I began to keep an accounting of my days: how I felt and what was occurring in my life. There seemed to be a direct correlation between my bad days and the amount of stress I was under. In addition, clearly, the less sleep I got the worse I felt. I found certain foods that had never bothered me before now caused painful and embarrassing digestive problems. I would break out in periods of sweat, sometimes drenching my pillow in my sleep. Doctors thought it was related to hormone levels, but tests showed nothing conclusive.

One test, however, showed elevated enzyme levels in my liver. I was referred to a liver specialist, who examined me and tested me further. He assumed that I was a heavy drinker and that I had severely damaged my liver with years of alcohol abuse. He found it puzzling when he discovered I had never consumed alcohol in excess. He then said he had a hunch that I probably had a tumor in my liver. He wanted to do a biopsy. Well, I was not letting anyone cut into my liver on a hunch!

Needless to say, all of this was very depressing. I had seen countless doctors and had been through a myriad of tests, spent thousands of dollars, and I was no closer to finding out what was wrong with me!

One day Ryne was visiting with a friend at his work. He described to this man what was happening to me. His friend suggested a doctor in Bellevue, Washington, who had helped him overcome some serious medical challenges. With this recommendation, Ryne and I researched the doctor and the clinic. We liked what we found, so we set off on a trip to Bellevue.

Dr. Boles was a medical doctor who had incorporated herbal and naturopathic treatments into his practice. His practice had been under scrutiny by the medical board in the state of Washington, because he believed in the body's ability to heal itself and he practiced some very unorthodox treatments. Ryne and I were perplexed with his diagnosis, yet he finally gave me one! His evidence-based diagnosis was complex. I was, according to Dr. Boles, suffering with chronic fatigue, fibromyalgia, irritable bowel syndrome, and a systemic yeast infection. One sounded bad enough—but all four at the same time!

Finally, someone had given a name to my demons, and I returned home to Montana to study and learn about these afflictions. I searched for any and all information that was available. I spent countless hours studying and reading case studies and reports. These conditions were strange and not well understood. Most medical professionals were skeptical, but there were thousands of folks suffering from symptoms similar to mine. No longer could the similarities be ignored, and herbalists and naturopaths were joining forces with the medical profession to help treat these mysterious illnesses.

In October of the following year, I went by myself back to the Boles Clinic in Bellevue. I stayed for a month with my ex-husband, Neil, and his wife, Kate, at their home in Bellevue. I underwent chelation therapy and peroxide treatments, formulated to rid my system of toxins so that my body could begin to heal itself. It was a long time to be away from Ryne. Megan was in her first year of post-secondary at The University of Washington in Seattle and Lauren was home in high school with Ryne.

When I did return to Missoula, feeling better, I made some long-term commitments to change my lifestyle in order to cope. Although not life threatening, these diagnoses would affect my quality of life, maybe forever!

I Don't Like Spiders or Snakes

Fall once again rolled around, and the morning air was crisp and clean. I was working as a real-estate agent in Missoula, and I had an early showing, so I was up and ready early. I jumped in my car and sped down the hill to town. I stopped at a red light and had just pulled through the intersection when a movement inside my car caught my eye. There, sprawled out on my gearshift, was a huge wooly spider. I screeched and quickly looked in my rearview mirror. Without even signaling, I swerved for the side of the road. I hurriedly opened the door and barreled out of the car. It must have been a sight to the oncoming morning traffic: a crazy woman jumping from her driver seat and then running around to the passenger side, screaming.

I opened the passenger door and grabbed my purse from the seat. Frantically, I searched for something to arm myself with. The only thing that I could find was my aerosol breath freshener. I grasped the small can and aimed. As a stream of spray covered the spider with a white, minty-fresh substance, it staggered and fell through the hole in the rubber gearshift cover. I waited for quite a while, and when it did not reappear, I figured I had killed it. With reluctance, I returned to my driver seat and continued on my way.

I still had plenty of time before my appointment, in spite of the recent event, so when I drove by the local car wash, I decided to vacuum and wash my car, so as to make a favorable impression with my new clients. First, I vacuumed the interior; then I paid the wash attendant and pulled in line for the wash. I glanced several times at the hole in the cover surrounding the shifter. The smell of mint still permeated the air, but there was no sign of the creepy spider. I applauded my quick response and my use of the breath spray to ward off the creature. I pulled forward and grabbed the gearshift, putting the car in neutral for the automatic car wash.

I was somewhere between the jetting spray of soap and the car wash octopus when it happened. The spider reemerged from its minty incarceration and positioned itself directly on my right knee. I saw it as I was wiping down the dash. Overwhelmed with fear, I scaled the seat in seconds, in a skirt and heels, no less. I screamed and thrashed about, bouncing the spider onto the floor mat below. Boobs, arms, legs, and butt were in motion, and I soon found myself sitting in my back seat, eyes still glued to the arachnid that was now motionless on the mat. The car inched forward as the rinse cycle commenced, but my eyes never left the spider.

My concentration was only broken by a knock on my window as two attendants shouted, "What's wrong, ma'am?" Oh God, it would appear that my car had no driver, and its occupant was in the back seat looking considerably disheveled.

I yelled to them, "Spider!"

The car jolted to a stop on the track, and one of the young men opened the back door. Still shaken, I tried to collect myself as I explained my dilemma and stepped out of the car. The other young man opened the driver's door, withdrew the mat, and stomped on the spider. He flicked it off the mat and replaced it as I regained my composure and murmured, "Ya'll have a nice day." Once again behind the wheel, I drove off, leaving the two of them dumbfounded and laughing.

I made my appointment that morning and even sold a house.

Damn spider, anyway!

And Then There Were None

I absolutely adored being a mom. I loved the time when my girls were babies, toddlers, pre-teens, and teens—and now that they are adults, I still love it! I view my experiences as a mother to be the most rewarding journeys in my life. I know I've made mistakes, but both of my girls love me, even in spite of the "mom-isms."

Megan was a wonderful child and a remarkable teenager and gave us very little grief in her growing years. I had prepared myself for Megan to leave home, but even though I was ready, I still had a difficult time when she finally packed her car to leave. It was only one day after her high-school graduation, and I was still high on the celebration when she began to haul boxes of her belongings to her car. I had to face the fact that she was really leaving. Her choice of post-secondary school took her to Seattle and to the University of Washington. Her father lived in the Seattle area, and having Neil close to Megan gave me a bit more peace of mind. I held my tears back until her little car was out of sight, but for the next several days I walked past her vacant room and cried. I missed her very much.

Megan had always been a very independent girl, in search of her identity as she filtered through her emotions and future prospects. Ryne and I, along with Neil, had certainly raised her the best we could. Now it would be important to sit back and allow her the opportunity to grow and make mistakes, as well as to celebrate her triumphs. We maintained a close relationship with her, and I delighted in the fact that she still called us now and then to ask our opinions about something. She did amazing things in college. Her grades were fantastic, and she was very involved in her acting. She surpassed every expectation we had ever had with regard to her scholastic abilities. Megan finished her undergraduate studies in four years; in fact, she graduated with two degrees, one in drama and one in English. And, she returned to further her education and attended law school at Seattle University.

Lauren was, and always will be, my diamond! She was such a sweet little girl, bright and expressive, and so very talented. She always loved to create things and had this wonderful uninhibited sense of style. With her beautiful auburn-red hair and eyes the color of sapphires, she turned heads from birth! She and I have always been very close, even while Megan was still home. Then, after Megan left home, our relationship became even closer. Lauren has always been kind and thoughtful, a good listener, a devoted sister, and a fabulous daughter. She has a quick wit, and I always have myself a good laugh when around her. However, she has a melancholy side too.

Lauren did well in grade school but had a tough time in high school. It seemed that she was too distracted with all of her creative juices. She was absolutely okay with getting mediocre marks in any of the subjects that just didn't stretch her imagination. It's not that she got bad grades—and the truth is that the kid was smart enough to excel in anything—but unless it motivated her and challenged her artistic side, she felt it was just a waste of her time. Like her sister, she was not afraid to voice her opinion, so she left home before her senior year in high school and moved to Seattle to live with her dad. She enrolled in a program offered in the state of Washington that allowed her to take college courses and still receive her high-school diploma. I envied her passion and adventuresome spirit at such a young age.

I was not as ready for this one to leave. It was just too soon and not a planned event. I guess I knew that when she packed up and was gone, I really would have to accept my life as an empty nester.

Epilogue

The comforting whistles of the train woke me, and as I stared at the ceiling, I thought to myself, "Well, it's just another day in paradise." The clock on the nightstand read four thirty. Wincing, I slowly stretched my arms and legs and waited for the pain to subside before quietly pushing back the comforter. I pulled myself up to sit on the edge of the bed, as my dogs began to emerge from underneath the covers. My husband stirred, rolled over in bed, and quickly resumed his snoring. I waited for the room to stop spinning before standing and herding the dogs toward the bedroom door. I grabbed my robe, slipped my feet into my slippers, and slowly moved to the top of the stairs. I turned on the light in the stairwell and waited for the dogs to scamper down before me. I carefully negotiated the steps, taking one at a time until I was safely at the bottom. I rounded the corner to the kitchen and turned on the coffeemaker. In the faint light, I led the dogs to the back door and then, slowly retracing my steps to the hallway, I flipped on the bathroom light.

The mirrored reflection before me no longer revealed a young, freckle-faced redheaded girl. I now saw a middle-aged woman who needed to shed a few extra pounds. My once-vibrant red hair had begun to fade, and as I brushed back the graying tendrils from my face, I noticed that, in addition to those few lingering freckles, I had acquired some new age spots on my hands. I peered at the mirror image looking back at me, stuck out my lower lip, and made a funny face. It's strange how the years flew by without me even noticing those wrinkles that had begun to appear around my eyes and mouth. Inching a bit closer to the image before me, I drew up the corners of my mouth until a smile emerged.

I continued on my regular morning routine, but this day felt different. I began to once again think about my life and what had brought me joy throughout the years. I saw a wife who has always been committed to her husband, a mother who still has an undying love for her children, a woman who admires and holds dear the relationship with her sisters, a daughter who misses her mother, and—oh my gosh—I'm a grandmother now!

I was reminded of how very fragile life is. I remembered the many loved ones I had lost over the years, and even though those losses were difficult, I find solace in my life. I don't dwell on loss; rather, I celebrate life. As a Christian, I believe in a life eternal; therefore, I accept as truth that the future is both for the living *and* the dead.

My dad is gone but certainly not forgotten. I still think about him and miss his wisdom, his humor, and his smile. I won't ever forget him, and I hope that the recollections I have shared in this book will help keep his memory alive for my daughters and for the rest of my family.

My memories of Grandma and Grandpa Clark live on. I remember them often, and I realize the value of their teachings and the rich significance of their presence in my life. They blessed me in so many ways.

Grandpa Stan died June 15, 1982, and Grandma Smith died twenty-eight years later, on July 19, 2010. Grandma was ninety-eight years old, and her weak little body just gave up. As God would have it, Momma was with Grandma as she drew her last breath. I will always remember Grandma as a gift from God. I am so fortunate to have had her in my life well into my fifties.

My brother, Phil, took his own life in 2008. I choose to remember him as a special man, devoted to his family and friends, rather than as an alcoholic who spun out of control. He was, and will always be, my prized baby brother.

I am close to my two sisters, Debbie and Pam. Pam and I are extremely close and me and my sister, Debbie have had a tumultuous relationship in recent years. I don't see them as often as I would like but we talk often. I live in Washington, Deb and Pam reside in Montana. We have been talking a lot more lately, as we deal with problems and situations concerning our aging mother.

It's been almost thirty-five + years since I had that conversation with my friend, Yvonne. She had insisted that Neil and I would never mend our relationship. Well, we proved her wrong. We share two beautiful daughters and have a mutual respect for one another. Sure, our divorce was hurtful. Life was painful for a while, but I believed that we could rise above our indifference, and we both did!

I have never regretted a single moment with my husband, Ryne. He and I will grow old together as we experience the many seasons of our lives. I just know that he will always be there for me and me for him. Oh sure, we have our spats. Mostly, I nag and he resists. I'm still trying to teach him a thing or two, but darn, he makes those lessons harder than they really need to be! We have been so blessed in our life together.

We have managed to completely renovate two houses without ending in divorce, built two new homes, become business partners, raise children and celebrate 35 years of marriage in September 2024. He is a self-taught carpenter, plumber, and electrician, and with my creative spirit and knack for landscape design and decorating, we have been very successful our home building endeavors.

We bought a fishing and wildlife ecotourism float lodge in British Columbia, Canada, in January 2010. Ryne completely renovated and remodeled the lodge, by himself, the first year we purchased the business. In recent years, we partnered in with an amazing couple and purchased two tourism businesses on North Vancouver Island, British Columbia, Canada. Ryne and I are apart for many months each year. It's tough. I am not gonna lie; with all of my health challenges that I face each and every day, it's really hard on me.

In addition to running our businesses in Canada, Ryne continues a successful career in the transportation industry, owning two businesses in Spokane, WA. He astounds me with his motivation and work ethic. He is my knight in shining armor; he simply never wavers.

Our four children are healthy and happy adults, each one with a promising future. After graduating from college, Megan worked in the service industry for seven years as a successful manager. With determination, she became a certified paralegal in 2008 and with gusto and grace, entered law school and graduated in the spring of 2011 with her juris doctorate degree. At the age of thirty-three, she became a public defender in Everett, Washington, and she continues to amaze me! Currently, she works for the State of Washington as a securities regulator, catching the "bad guys," who commit securities fraud. She is so intelligent and continues to rise to each challenge in her life with Montana grit.

Lauren obtained her associates degree and currently is managing a large Airbnb with her dad and step-mom in Poulsbo, WA. She managed a restaurant in the Seattle area and even owned her own cleaning business for a time. She continues to hone her artistic talents. Lauren persists to chisel away pieces of her protective armor, only to reveal what I've known was there all the time, a sparkling diamond! She remains strong-minded and is learning to accept her strengths and weaknesses. She is continually seeking knowledge and keeps dangling the carrot of further education in front of herself. When she figures out where she wants to be in life, the world had better watch out!

Natashia completed her schooling in cosmetology and is now a hairstylist and owns her own salon in Windsor, Ontario, Canada. She leads a very busy lifestyle, and because of the miles between us, we don't get to see her very often. She is married now and she and her husband have a beautiful little girl, Ellianna, who is the apple of her grandpa Ryne's eye.

Nathan spent four years serving in the United States Navy, aboard the Abraham Lincoln, after which he moved up the ladder in a car dealership in Spokane, Washington. In 2008, he blessed us with a beautiful grandson, Zachary Ryne. He and his wife divorced in 2012, but we are close to him and love to spend time with our little grandson at every opportunity we have. Nathan remarried in 2019 and he and his wife blessed us with another grandson, Sullivan in 2020. He is absolutely precious.

I retired from working outside the home in 2009 and am now a domestic engineer—which is just a fancy name for a stay-at-homer. I delight in the care and organization of our home, and I continue to nurture my creativity by reading, scrapbooking, decorating, crafting, gardening, painting, and writing.

Still struggling with my health issues, I fight to keep my body going. In 1992 I was involved in a very serious car collision that caused trauma to my right shoulder and my right knee and my face. In addition to my 1996 diagnosis of fibromyalgia and chronic fatigue, I was diagnosed with type 2 diabetes in 2001. In November of 2002, I got braces to begin to correct an unusual growth occurring in my upper as a result of the car accident in 1992. Still with a mouthful full of metal, I had upper jaw surgery to shave the upper jaw bone. I remained in braces until September of 2005. Following that surgery, all of my teeth started dying due to trauma and the restorative surgery was extensive. Even now, my teeth are failing and I just keep repairing. I guess I have the "million dollars," smile. Truth is, not many of my teeth haven't been ground down, built up, drilled on, fortified and/or duplicated. Ryne and I could've traveled the world on what the dentists, endodontists, and orthodontists have made on me over the years.

In 2008 I had the first of two surgeries on my feet to treat Morton's neuromas, a very painful nerve condition. That condition, my fellow citizens, is a direct result of me wearing high fricking heals in my pageant years and while singing in a band. Crap! If only I would have known!

September 2013 was absolutely terrifying. I ended up in the ER with a serious bout of diverticulitis. They ordered a CT scan and when that scan was read, they discovered oversized lymph nodes deep in my abdomen. The ER physician referred me to an oncologist at Cancer Care Northwest in Spokane, WA. A day later I was laying on my stomach in an exam room, peering through a hole in a face rest while they performed a very painful bone biopsy on my spine. Then, off to have a PET scan. The PET scan indicated that I had lymphoma and the "hot spots," in my lungs, chest, and neck were indicators of where they believed the "cancer," started. CANCER! Geeze! Words that not a single person wants to hear. The oncologist told Ryne and me that the PET scan made my insides light up like a Christmas tree. The physicians ordered biopsies, a lung wash, and lots of blood work. We were told that it may be a while before they would have anything conclusive of when and what treatment would be required to fight the cancer; they believed it was Stage 3 or maybe even Stage 4.

The very next day, Ryne and I made the trip to Montana to tell my sisters and my mom. It was a pretty somber day. They asked a lot of questions that we really didn't have the information available to us yet. We told them what we knew, which was not much, other than I had been diagnosed with cancer.

The following weeks were spent in absolute agony! I had a total of 4 attempted biopsies of lymph nodes in several different locations. The lymph nodes were hardened and it was impossible to get the biopsy needle to penetrate them. Finally, the 5th attempt, a biopsy of a node behind my left clavicle bone was successful. But there were NO cancer cells present. Absolutely none!

Sitting back in the office of the oncologist, it was explained to Ryne and me that I did not, in fact have lymphoma… cancer, as I had been misdiagnosed. What I did have was a non-curable disease known as Sarcoidosis, a rare condition that was ravaging my body and mimicked lymphoma in this early stage. So, for almost a month, I believe that I had stage 3 or possibly even stage 4 lung cancer, that had more than likely metastasized. Really awful!!

Suffering from 2010 thru 2015 with chronic diverticulitis, a surgeon finally recommended that I have my sigmoid colon removed. It was a miserable recovery and during that time, I became very withdrawn. In addition, approximately one year following that surgery, I developed a very serious incisional hernia. Basically, I developed a bulge low on my abdomen that looked like I was ready to give birth to an alien. I joked with family and friends about my condition but it was actually very embarrassing and just made me withdraw further from the public.

Then came my frightening, "real" cancer diagnosis on September 12, 2019, that of breast cancer. To be honest with y'all, I handled the news pretty well. Ryne and I just faced it head on. But I also had to face this…3 weeks prior to the cancer diagnosis, I underwent the surgery to repair that horrible hernia. The surgery, first thought to be successful, went horribly wrong. I wound up in the operating room only a week after for a second surgery to address a very dangerous infection. My body had rejected some of the internal sutures and I had developed a staph infection very deep in my abdomen. I was hospitalized following that second surgery and was outfitted with a "wound care vac," before being discharged from the hospital a week later. At home, I was hooked up to this machine that pumped out the infection and was going to help the wound, (incision) heal, and rid my body of the staff infection. That frickin' thing had to go everywhere with me. And, I mean EVERYWHERE!

Home-health-care nurses visited me every day to repack the wound and they attempted to keep my spirits up. I only slipped further and further into a very deep depression. With my breast surgery on hold until my abdominal wound healed, I faced the deepest, darkest depression imaginable. Well, for me anyway.

It soon became apparent that my wound was not healing quick enough and my breast surgeon finally was forced to make the decision to operate with this machine placed on the gurney with me…situated right between my legs. So, off to the operating room. I had breast surgery and underwent radiation treatments. Surgery and recovery weren't exactly a piece of cake but you know, it just needed to be dealt with. After the 5-year mark from surgery and treatment, I was cancer free.

In the many years of battling my illnesses, I have learned to accept them. The fibromyalgia symptoms never go away; they're constant, and I don't take for granted the good days. The Sarcoidosis has ravaged my body. I am severely immunocompromised. The disease has affected several organs throughout my body; my lungs, kidneys, liver, bladder, nerves, eyes, and skin. The outward signs of the disease are hard to accept. I have terrible scaring on my face, legs, knees and elbows. Sarcoidosis "granulomas," attacked any scars on my body. In my younger days, that fall from my bicycle that left a scar, is now further scar and that scar is a constant reminder that I have this "thing," living inside of me. The disease causes disfiguring scars…blisters that ooz fluid and so very painful. It's like having perpetual shingles, which I have had recently.

I no longer have the lung capacity to sing as well, walk as well or even laugh as loud. I experience extreme fatigue and exhaustion most days. I have, what I call "mental dullness." Covid put me in the hospital twice! I did not fair too well having contracted that nasty virus, now 2 different times. I have had 5 surgical procedures to drain fluid from under my lungs, have had 2 collapsed lungs, 6 lithotripsy procedures to break up kidney stones, 5 ambulance rides to the hospital, and a frickin', "partridge in a pear tree." I gotta laugh!

However, I do have really good days. Those are the days that I drink in all that comes my way and try to laugh in the face of adversity. Some of my days are certainly better than others. There are many things that I simply cannot do any more, and I get frustrated at how my body responds to my demands. I try not to let these demons control me, but I am well aware that they are always with me. I pray for a cure or a remedy that will give me a better quality of life, but until then I try to live each day to the fullest.

I will never stop hoping or dreaming. I will never stop changing, and I'm afraid that I will never stop making mistakes, either. I just hope that I continue to learn from them. I will always look for the good in people, and I will treasure the simple things in life. I desire to live my life to the fullest, and I look around the corner, with anticipation, for the next adventure I will encounter.

So, these are some of my stories. I still have so many stories in my arrow quiver. Maybe I need to write a sequel to Under the Apple Tree? The writing of this book gave me the courage to look again at my past as well as the wisdom to accept things and move on with my life. The really glorious outcome of this entire experience is that I began to love my memories again, including the painful ones. I have learned to accept the broken promises, the unfulfilled dreams, and even the dreams left simmering. I fondly remember that lesson from long ago when Daddy told me that I needed to nurture the seeds of change. Metaphorically, I sit under my apple tree and am awestruck at the world around me. Through the ebb and flow of life, I am always reminded that you only need a seed to begin again.

35 years of marriage, 2024

Ryne, Rebecca and their beloved pets Emmylou and Teddy at Alder Bay Resort and Marina, North Vancouver Island, British Columbia, Canada

Rebecca, laughing wearing her "Woodstock wannabe," wig as she celebrates another glorious day!

www.ingramcontent.com/pod-product-compliance
Lightning Source LLC
Chambersburg PA
CBHW060553080526
44585CB00013B/551